COLORADO
WILDLIFE
VIEWING GUIDE

SECOND EDITION REVISED

Mary Taylor Young, Author

Janine "Robin" Hernbrode, Project Manager

Paul Gray, Illustrations

Watchable Wildlife, Inc.

ACKNOWLEDGMENTS

This book is a cooperative effort of the agencies who serve as stewards of the state's land and its wild residents: the Colorado Division of Wildlife, the Colorado Wildlife Heritage Foundation, Colorado State Parks, the USDA Forest Service, the Bureau of Land Management, the U.S. Fish and Wildlife Service, and the Bureau of Reclamation.

Thank you Renée Herring and Teresa Burkert for all their hard work on this revised second edition reprint. Special thanks for bringing the second edition of the *Colorado Wildlife Viewing Guide* to fruition go to Steering Committee members Bob Hernbrode, Colorado Division of Wildlife; Faye Koeltzow, State Parks; Lee Upham, Bureau of Land Management; Darrell Cauley, Bureau of Reclamation; Melvie Uhland, U.S. Fish and Wildlife Service; Natasha Goedert, U.S. Forest Service; and Ed Alexander, Colorado Wildlife Heritage Foundation, who labored through long hours of site selection, organization, production, and review. A thank you goes to the dozens of BLM, Forest Service, State Parks, Bureau of Reclamation, U.S. Fish and Wildlife Service, and Division of Wildlife field employees, the people who know these special places best, who made key contributions to site selection and content review. Special thanks go to Marty Bates, Rose Bayless, Jeff Blake, Rex Brady, John Brandstatter, Martie Brean, Ken Brink Jr., Brad Buckner, Gary Buffington, Max Canestorp, Leonard Coleman, Tim Crisman, Warren Cummings, Ron DellaCroce, Jim Dennis, Rich Dudley, Deb Duke, Janet Ekstrum, Michelle Ellis, Julie Farrell, Bob Finch, Pete Firmin, Chris Foreman, Paul Foutz, Mike French, Anthony Garcia, Terry Gimbel, John Gray, Larry Green, Vic Grizzle, Julie Grode, Karen Hardesty, Del Holtz, Kay Hopkins, Tom Johnston, Terry Keane, Larry Kontour, John Koshak, Larry Kramer, Ron Lambeth, Carol Leasure, Steve McCall, Dave Meline, Judy Morse, John Nahomenuk, Gregg Nootbaar, Russ Pallone, Karen Rhoads, Jeff Riddle, Ron Rivale, Mark Robertson, Scott Roush, Dennis Scheiwe, Chris Schultz, Doug Secrist, Kathy Seiple, Mike Severin, Laura Smart, Tim Snowden, Dave Spencer, Brad Taylor, Kevin Tobey, Christine Torres, Susie Trumble, Will Tulley, Dave Uphoff, Dan Weber, John Weiss, Steve Werner, Rob White, Mike Widler, Bob Wiig, Scott Wilber, National Park Service personnel, and all BLM Field Office Wildlife Biologists. Special recognition to Richard L. Watson, Colorado State Office, BLM, for his cartography work.

Thank you to Shearer Publishing which allowed use of its excellent maps from *The Roads of Colorado*. Many of the base maps were traced from *The Roads of Colorado* published by Shearer Publishing, Fredericksburg, Texas.

© 2007 by Watchable Wildlife, Inc.
Printed in Korea

1 2 3 4 5 6 7 8 9 10 CE 04 03 02 01 00

Author: Mary Taylor Young • Project Manager: Janine "Robin" Hernbrode • Illustration: Paul Gray
Base maps traced from *The Roads of Colorado* published by Shearer Publishing, Fredericksburg, Texas.

Library of Congress Cataloging-in-Publication Data
Young, Mary Taylor, 1955-
    Colorado Wildlife Viewing Guide / by Mary Taylor Young.—Revised 2nd ed.
    p. cm.
    ISBN 1-56044-797-4 (pbk.)
    1. Wildlife viewing sites—Colorado—Guidebooks. 2. Wildlife watching—Colorado—Guidebooks. 3. Colorado—Guidebooks.
    QL165.Y68 2000
    599'.09788—dc21   99-089466
                                                                        CIP

A simple mission statement for a complex challenge; Watchable Wildlife Inc. is an independent nonprofit working with communities and state and federal wildlife agencies across North America. We help these agencies and organizations better utilize their wildlife and wild places.

To help communities and wildlife prosper

We accomplish this mission by developing sustainable wildlife viewing programs with our partners. Our areas of focus are our annual conference, publications and on-the-ground projects.

Our annual Watchable Wildlife Conference is the nation's best vehicle for presenting new ideas. It also serves as an international forum for training and recognizing the works of professionals in the field of wildlife viewing. Watchable Wildlife Inc. works hands-on with conservation-minded partners on projects across the continent to develop safe, satisfying and sustainable wildlife viewing.

Our Viewing Guide Series is a continent-wide effort to meet the needs of North America's growing wildlife viewing public. The guides encourage people to observe wildlife in natural settings and provides them with information on where to go, when to go, and what to expect when they get there. We believe the presence of wildlife viewing sites near communities has positive social and economic impacts.

We want wildlife viewing to be fun. However, we also believe it should be an economically viable resource for the host community. In the larger context, we want people to learn about wildlife, to care about it and to conserve it.

For more information about Watchable Wildlife Inc., this year's conference, our other publications and our current projects, visit www.watchablewildlife.org.

Looking for wildlife?
Look for these highway signs.

As you travel across Colorado, look for these special highway signs that identify wildlife viewing sites.

In most cases, these signs mark the location of sites described in this book. However, some signs are located at road intersections to indicate the route to a site or you may find signs for new sites created after this guide was published. For more information, visit www.wildlife.state.co.us/viewing.

CONTENTS

FRONT RANGE

ROCKY MOUNTAINS

COLORADO PLATEAU

A group of birdwatchers searches for songbirds in a cottonwoodland along a stream. They, and millions like them, are participating in wildlife watching, a popular and growing activity. W. PERRY CONWAY

INTRODUCTION

Without wildlife, Colorado would be an infinitely less enchanting place to live. From its broad prairies to the tops of its 14,000-foot peaks, Colorado is defined by its more than 960 species of wildlife. Wildlife is so much a part of our lives that we take for granted the hawk circling above a prairie dog colony or the elk grazing in a mountain meadow. Wildlife thrives in our state, and it is possible to see wildlife almost everywhere. The *Colorado Wildlife Viewing Guide* is designed to provide you with the opportunity to find new places to see and enjoy a wide variety of wild species. As you enjoy Colorado's wildlife, we hope you will come to better understand and appreciate this precious natural heritage so that our children and grandchildren will have the same opportunities.

The Watchable Wildlife program of the Colorado Division of Wildlife is funded primarily by Great Outdoors Colorado monies from the Colorado Lottery, not by hunting and fishing license revenues. No general tax dollars are used for the Colorado Division of Wildlife budget.

PROJECT SPONSORS

The BUREAU OF LAND MANAGEMENT is responsible for the stewardship of 8.3 million acres of public lands in Colorado. The Bureau is committed to managing, protecting, and improving these lands in a manner to serve the needs of the American people. Management is based on the principles of multiple use and sustained yield of our nation's renewable and non-renewable resources within a framework of environmental responsibility and scientific technology. The vast majority of BLM-administered lands are located in the Colorado Plateau and Rocky Mountain regions of Colorado. The Bureau's Watchable Wildlife program provides the opportunity to view wildlife on these public lands. Bureau of Land Management, Colorado State Office, 2850 Youngfield St., Lakewood, CO 80215. 303-239-3600. **www.co.blm.gov**

The BUREAU OF RECLAMATION was created by the Reclamation Act of 1902 to reclaim arid lands for agriculture in the seventeen western states. Today, the Bureau of Reclamation's mission has evolved to meet the increasing water demands of the West while protecting the environment and the public's investment. Projects include water conservation, irrigation, hydroelectric power production, wetlands preservation, and recreation. In Colorado, the Bureau of Reclamation has 347,000 acres of land on which 31 dams and reservoirs are located. These reservoirs encompass 50,423 surface acres of water and 518 shoreline miles which provide habitat to a variety of Colorado's wildlife. Bureau of Reclamation, Denver Office, Denver Federal Center, Denver, CO 80225. 303-445-2797. **www.usbr.gov**

The COLORADO DIVISION OF WILDLIFE's mission is to protect and enhance the wildlife resources of the state and provide an opportunity for people to enjoy them. Wildlife makes a fundamental contribution to the quality of life in Colorado, both aesthetically and economically. Wildlife management is the tool the Division uses to enhance this quality of life. Participation in this publication is part of the Division's ongoing efforts to help people better enjoy wildlife. Colorado Division of Wildlife, 6060 Broadway, Denver, CO 80216. 303-297-1192. **www.wildlife.state.co.us**

DEFENDERS OF WILDLIFE is a national, nonprofit organization of more than 80,000 members and supporters dedicated to preserving the natural abundance and diversity of wildlife and its habitat. A one-year membership is $25 and includes six issues of the bimonthly magazine Defenders. To join or for further information, write or call Defenders of Wildlife, 1130 17th Street, NW, Washington, DC 20036. 800-385-9712. **www.defenders.org**

 The COLORADO WILDLIFE HERITAGE FOUNDATION is a non-profit organization committed to protecting and enhancing Colorado's wildlife resources. The Foundation serves as a repository for land donations, financial gifts, and membership dues, and puts them to work to assure that Colorado's wildlife thrives. Colorado Wildlife Heritage Foundation, P.O. Box 211512, Denver, CO 80221. 303-291-7212. **www.wildlife.state.co.us/cwhf**

 The USDA FOREST SERVICE manages 16 million acres of wildlife habitat in Colorado under a mandate to protect, improve and wisely use the nation's natural resources for multiple purposes. The seven national forests and two national grasslands in Colorado are sponsors of this program to promote the fish and wildlife on national forest service lands. For further information on national forest opportunities in Colorado, contact: USDA Forest Service, Rocky Mountain Region, 740 Simms St., Golden, CO 80401. 303-275-5350. **www.fs.fed.us**

 The U.S. FISH AND WILDLIFE SERVICE's mission is to conserve, protect, and enhance fish, wildlife, and plants and their habitats for the continuing benefit of the American people. The Service works with many partners—federal and state agencies, tribal and local governments and communities, conservation organizations, and individual citizens—to manage America's wildlife and habitat resources. Major responsibilities include migratory birds, endangered species, and inland fisheries management. In Colorado, the Service administers six National Wildlife Refuges and two National Fish Hatcheries. U.S. Fish and Wildlife Service, P.O. Box 25486, Denver Federal Center, Denver, CO 80225. 303-236-7905. **www.fws.gov**

 The mission of COLORADO STATE PARKS is to be leaders in providing outdoor recreation through the stewardship of Colorado's natural resources for the enjoyment, education and inspiration of present and future generations. Funding from the Watchable Wildlife in Parks (WWIP) program and Great Outdoors Colorado (GOCO) has been used to provide new ways to view and understand wildlife at each park. Colorado State Parks, 1313 Sherman Street, Room 618, Denver, CO 80203. 303-866-3437. **www.parks.state.co.us**

 The mission of GREAT OUTDOORS COLORADO (GOCO) is to help preserve, protect, enhance, and manage the state's wildlife, park, river, trail and open space heritage. GOCO receives approximately 50% of the proceeds from the Colorado Lottery and awards grants, including through the Colorado Division of Wildlife, to preserve and protect Colorado's wildlife and its habitat, and to provide wildlife viewing opportunities, information and education. Purchase of lottery tickets, including Powerball tickets, benefits wildlife. Great Outdoors Colorado, 1600 Broadway, Suite 1650, Denver, CO 80202. 303-863-7522 **www.goco.org**

This is Colorado

Paul Gray © 1999

13

STATE MAP

This guide is divided into four geographic regions, covering the state from east to west. Eastern Plains includes the state's prairie region from the Kansas border to the edge of the mountains. Front Range covers the rapidly growing, high-population urban corridor where the High Plains meet the mountains. Rocky Mountains includes the central, mountainous part of the state. Colorado Plateau encompasses the plateau region of western Colorado.

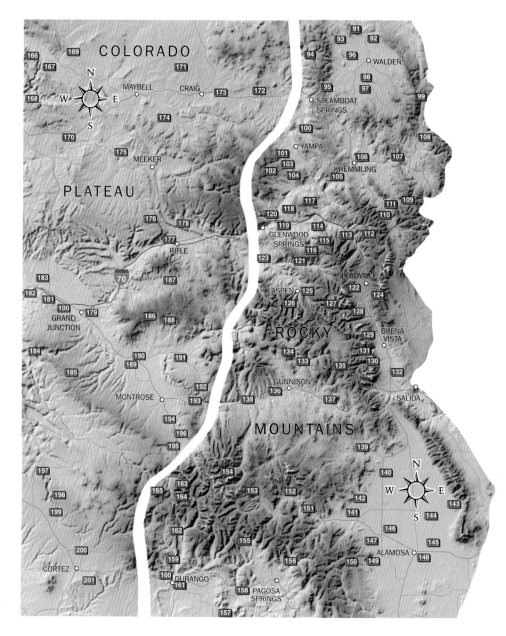

165	Site Number
P	Parking
T	Trailhead
⋯	Trail
△	Campground
	Urban Area
C 14	Colorado State Hwy
69	County Roads
76	US Highway
25	Interstate Highway

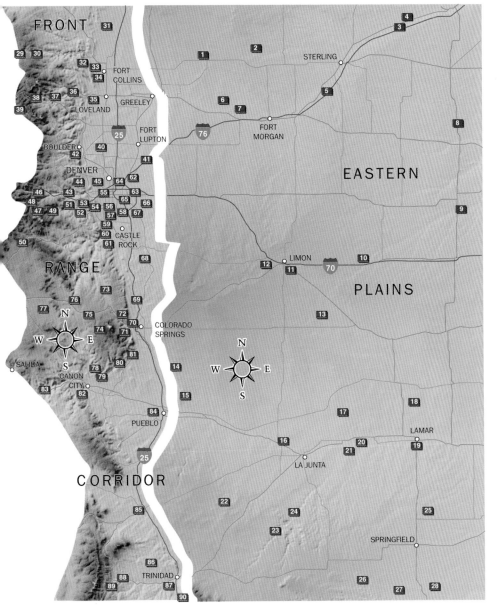

FRONT

RANGE

CORRIDOR

EASTERN

PLAINS

VIEWING HINTS AND OUTDOOR ETHICS

A few tips to increase your viewing success while not disturbing wildlife:

Time your outing for morning and evening, when wildlife are most active.

Keep your distance, for the safety and comfort of both animals and people. If an animal changes its behavior, stops feeding or otherwise seems nervous at your presence, it's time to back away.

Use binoculars, spotting scopes and long lenses for a closeup view.

Avoid disturbing wildlife by **moving slowly and quietly**. Noise and quick movements mean "danger" to wildlife. They may run or fly off, sometimes leaving nests and young unprotected.

Find a likely spot for animal activity, then sit quietly and wait for wildlife to emerge. You'll have a better chance of observing the animals' natural behavior.

Wear earth-tone clothes, like gray, khaki and olive-green. Animals will tolerate you better if you blend into the surroundings.

Use your car as a viewing blind.

Share snacks with people, not wildlife. Human food is not healthy for wild animals. Feeding animals changes their behavior in ways that can be harmful to them, and to people.

Learn more about wildlife, and what you can expect to see where, by consulting a field guide or other resource before you go. Then bring the guide along to help identify what you see.

KEY TO ICONS

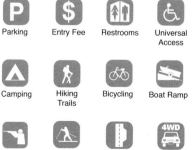

Parking	Entry Fee	Restrooms	Universal Access	Picnic	Water
Camping	Hiking Trails	Bicycling	Boat Ramp	Fishing	Horse Trails
Hunting	Cross-Country Skiing	Road Pullout	4WD	Auto Tour	Habitat Stamp

HOW TO USE THIS GUIDE

The wildlife viewing sites in this guide are grouped into four geographic regions—Eastern Plains, Front Range, Rocky Mountains, and Colorado Plateau. Each site profile includes a description of the site's habitat, vegetation and landscape, what wildlife to watch for, and facilities or special information for the site. Icons indicate ways to explore the site (hike, auto tour, etc.), if there is an entry fee, on-site facilities such as parking, universal access, restrooms, water, camping, trails, picnic, or boat ramp, and allowed activities like bicycling, cross-country skiing, and hunting. To clarify if your activity is appropriate at the time you plan to be there, please call the telephone number provided for the site. Since hunting regulations may change every year, check the DOW website for the most current information concerning hunting at a particular site. Also shown are the size of the site, the managing agency, a telephone number where additional site information may be obtained, and the nearest town, with mileage to it, if applicable. Restaurant and lodging icons refer to services available in that town. Point-to-point auto tours and sites in-town do not show distances to the nearest town. A map indicates how to reach the site. However, use of an additional road atlas or other map is strongly recommended.

Site Owner/Manager Abbreviations
BLM – Bureau of Land Management
BOR – Bureau of Reclamation
CDOT – Colorado Department of Transportation
CDOW – Colorado Division of Wildlife
CSU – Colorado State University
CWHF – Colorado Wildlife Heritage Foundation
DMNS – Denver Museum of Nature & Science
NPS – National Park Service
PVT – Private ownership
RMBO – Rocky Mountain Bird Observatory
State Parks – Colorado State Parks
TNC – The Nature Conservancy
USFS – USDA Forest Service
USFWS – U.S. Fish and Wildlife Service

Websites
- Bureau of Land Management: www.co.blm.gov
- Colorado Division of Wildlife website: www.wildlife.state.co.us; specific wildlife viewing information, visit www.wildlife.state.co.us/viewing
- Colorado Scenic Byways: www.coloradobyways.org
- Colorado State Parks website: www.parks.state.co.us; individual park websites can be accessed through the general web site.
- Colorado Tourism Office: www.colorado.com
- National Park Service: www.nps.gov
- USDA Forest Service: www.fs.fed.us
- U.S. Fish and Wildlife Service: www.fws.gov

Maps

More detailed maps than the site maps in this book are recommended to help you locate the viewing sites. Consult your local map or bookstore, or contact the following agencies.

Maps and information on state parks are available for free by calling the State Parks' Denver Administration Office at 303-866-3437, or on the State Parks website.

Color-coded maps showing land ownership, topography, roads and landscape features for all of Colorado can be purchased at any Bureau of Land Management office. Check **www.blm.gov** for office locations and phone numbers or call the Denver-area BLM office at 303-239-3600.

Maps of national forests are available at USDA Forest Service offices and at outdoor recreation retailers, map shops, and some bookstores.

Download national park maps on the internet at **www.nps.gov/carto**

Camping Reservations/Information

For State Parks campground reservations, call 303-470-1144 during regular business hours, or reserve online at the State Parks website. Campground information and fees are also on the website.

Reservations for USDA Forest Service campgrounds can be made ahead through the National Recreation Reservation System at 877-444-6777 or on the internet at **www.reserveusa.com**.

Reservations for National Park campgrounds can be made by calling 800-365-CAMP (ext. 2267) or on the internet at **www.reservations.nps.gov**.

HABITAT STAMP — For State Wildlife Areas

A habitat stamp is required to access State Wildlife Areas or State Trust Lands. It is automatically purchased with each DOW hunting or fishing license, at an additional cost of $5 per license. It can be purchased without buying a license for $10.25 wherever hunting and fishing licenses are sold, online through the DOW Total Licensing System, or by calling 800-244-5613. For more information, visit **www.wildlife.state.co.us**.

COLORADO BIRDING TRAIL

The Colorado Birding Trail is a series of drives, loops and viewing stops that offer particularly good opportunities to see birds and other wildlife. First developed in southeastern Colorado, the trail will eventually encompass the entire state. For more information, visit **www.coloradobirdingtrail.com**. Watch the birding trail grow across Colorado!

Eastern Plains

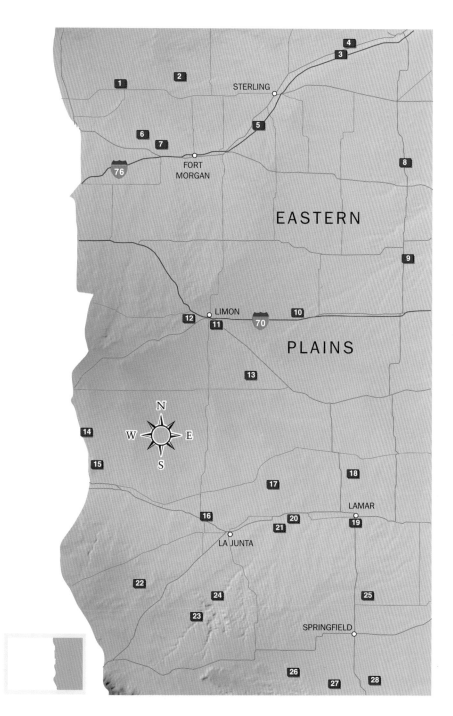

STERLING

FORT
MORGAN

EASTERN

LIMON

PLAINS

N
W E
S

LAMAR

LA JUNTA

SPRINGFIELD

With few trees to offer cover and nesting places, Colorado's Eastern Plains are home to prairie dogs, coyotes, pronghorn, burrowing owls, meadowlarks and other animals adapted to life in open country where little grows taller than the

Paul Gray ©1999

height of a person. Only about 10 percent of native shortgrass prairie survives, most of it now converted to farm fields and grazing pasture. Ribbons of woodlands mark streams and rivers.

Description: A premier prairie birdwatching tour; the bird checklist includes almost 300 species, including grassland birds, migrant waterfowl, and shorebirds. The cottonwood/willow riparian area at the Crow Valley Campground is like an oasis amid the dry shortgrass prairie, attracting a variety of eastern and mountain birds. The brochure "Birding on the Pawnee by Automobile or Mountain Bike" is available from the Pawnee National Grassland Headquarters, 660 "O" Street, Greeley, Colorado 80631. **www.fs.fed.us**

Viewing information: Good chance to see and hear "skylarking" (singing courtship flight) of lark buntings, horned larks, meadowlarks, and longspurs late May through June. Prairie birds to watch for include mountain plovers, chestnut-collared and McCown's longspurs, burrowing owls, and long-billed curlews. In the campground, streamside riparian habitat attracts a great variety of birds April through June and late August through October, including warblers, thrushes, flycatchers, orioles, and kingbirds. Murphy Reservoir offers good shorebird and waterfowl viewing.

Ownership: USFS (970-353-5004), PVT

Size: 36-mile self-guided tour

Closest town: Briggsdale, 2 miles

Directions: See map this page

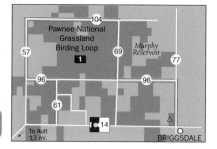

The long-billed curlew's in-flight cry sounds just like its name. The curlew's long, curved beak enables it to probe through sand and mud for crustaceans, mollusks, insects, and worms. W. PERRY CONWAY

Description: The Pawnee National Grassland is a remnant of the plains grassland that once covered eastern Colorado. Federal lands are intermingled with private ownership, and some blocks are grazed and cultivated. A USFS map of the grasslands, available at USFS offices in Colorado, is recommended to help distinguish between public and private lands. Dramatic high points are the Pawnee Buttes, a pair of sandstone formations towering 250 feet above the surrounding prairie. The grassland is divided into two parcels, with buttes in the eastern parcel. www.fs.fed.us

Viewing information: Such raptors as kestrels, prairie falcons, golden eagles, and Swainson's and ferruginous hawks nest on surrounding escarpments in isolated trees, and on the steep sides of the buttes. **Do not climb on the buttes or escarpments during sensitive nesting periods from early spring through mid-summer.** Watch for pronghorn, mule deer, coyotes, prairie dogs, jackrabbits, and kangaroo rats (at night). Grassland reptiles include short-horned lizards, bullsnakes, fence lizards, and western rattlesnakes. Excellent mammal fossils dating from the Miocene and Oligocene periods have been found at the buttes. **Fossils and cultural artifacts are protected by federal law.**

Ownership: PVT, USFS (970-353-5004)

Size: 693,060 acres

Closest town: New Raymer, 20 miles; restaurant

Directions: See map this page

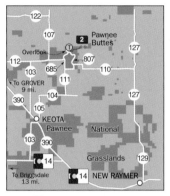

The Pawnee Buttes stand sentinel over northeast Colorado's Pawnee National Grassland. Premier bird watching country, the grassland preserves remnants of the once vast shortgrass prairie. SHERM SPOELSTRA

Found primarily on the state's eastern plains, the white-tailed deer is highly adaptable, but prefers the cover offered by wooded areas. When alarmed, the animal raises its tail like a flag as it flees. CLAUDE STEELMAN

3. TAMARACK RANCH STATE WILDLIFE AREA

Description: This site encompasses nearly 15 miles of the South Platte River and a variety of habitats—wooded bottomlands, farmed plots, and sagebrush sandhills. A portion of the grain cut on the plots is left for wildlife. Construction efforts are underway to create a series of open water ponds for management of native minnow species and to create critical wintering and spring nesting habitat for shorebirds and waterfowl. This is part of an interstate project and will continue for several years. **www.wildlife.state.co.us**

Viewing information: In early morning watch for greater prairie-chickens, a Colorado grouse recently taken off of the state endangered species list through reintroductions by the CDOW in the uplands on the south side of Interstate 76. Plains sharp-tailed grouse, another species endangered in Colorado, are returning naturally. Good site for wood ducks, bobwhite quail, and wild turkeys. Watch also for buntings, yellow- and black-billed cuckoos, Bell's vireos, grassland songbirds, and several grosbeaks. Watch for both western and eastern races of some species such as Bullock's orioles and common flickers. U.S. Highway 138 east of Crook may be the best spot in the state to see upland sandpipers. White-tailed deer along river bottoms. Duck Creek State Wildlife Area is nearby.

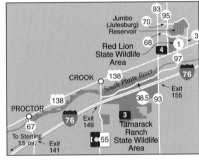

Ownership: CDOW (970-842-6300)

Size: 11,600 acres

Closest town: Crook, 2 miles; lodging

Directions: See map this page

4. RED LION/JUMBO RESERVOIR STATE WILDLIFE AREA

Description: Jumbo Reservoir and the Red Lion State Wildlife Area are surrounded by shortgrass prairie, mud flats, lowland marsh areas, and cottonwood riparian zones. Food plots and shelter belts have been established for upland birds and small mammals. Red Lion is closed during waterfowl nesting, late spring to early summer. **www.wildlife.state.co.us**

Viewing information: Excellent viewing of waterfowl in winter; three teal species seen in spring; Canada, snow, and occasional Ross's and white-fronted geese. Bald eagles and several gull species can be seen in winter. Sandhill cranes visible during spring and fall migrations. Watch for painted turtles. Upland sandpipers fairly common.

Ownership: CDOW (970-842-6300) • **Size:** 1,498 acres

Closest town: Crook, 9 miles; restaurant, lodging • *Directions: See map above*

Description: Grassland and old cultivated fields surround the reservoir, with patches of cottonwoods along the shore. Lowered water levels in dry years expose a sandy beach that can provide good habitat for shorebirds. www.wildlife.state.co.us

Viewing information: A good spot to see white pelicans, sometimes hundreds at once. Many great blue herons, coots, and ducks. Check the shoreline cottonwoods for flickers, red-headed woodpeckers, kingbirds, and a variety of songbirds. Watch for sandhill cranes stopping to feed and rest here during migrations. Bald eagles use the area in winter.

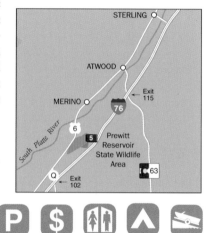

Ownership: CDOW (970-842-6300)

Size: 2,900 acres

Closest town: Merino, 4 miles

Directions: See map this page

The coot, a common sight around ponds and marshes, pumps its head back and forth while swimming. The white-billed bird dives below the surface of the water to feed or escape intruders.
TOM TIETZ

EASTERN PLAINS

Description: Plains reservoir surrounded by grasslands and fields with scattered cottonwoods and sandy beaches along the shore. **www.parks.state.co.us**

Viewing information: The reservoir is a major stopover for migrant shorebirds, bald eagles, waterfowl, and other water birds, especially white pelicans. Watch fields along the east side of the reservoir for sandhill cranes in spring and fall. Large groups of as many as 400 white pelicans can be seen during migration. Watch for shore and wading birds, gulls, and waterfowl, especially in dry years when lowered water levels expose sandy beaches and mud flats. Occasional duck flocks numbering 20,000 birds. Major bald eagle site with excellent viewing opportunities in the spring. Sometimes as many as forty will gather in February and March when the birds are preparing to migrate. Grassland areas attract plovers, longspurs, and horned larks. Numerous deer can be seen year-round.

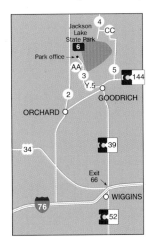

Ownership: State Parks (970-645-2551)

Size: 2,540 acres

Closest town: Wiggins, 12.5 miles

Directions: *See map this page*

Nesting colonies of white pelicans have established themselves throughout Colorado. Sound management practices resulted in population growth of the big-billed birds, and white pelicans have been removed from the state's endangered species list.
HARRY ENGELS

Description: The wide, sandy channel of the South Platte River—usually shallow except in spring—meanders across the High Plains of northeastern Colorado, supporting a lowland riparian community of cottonwoods, willows, hawthorns, wild currants, and wild plums, interspersed with cattail marshes.

Viewing information: A prime winter viewing site for bald eagles. Watch for the large, white-headed shapes of mature eagles roosting in the bare branches of cottonwoods. Immature eagles are similar in size but are mottled brown with dark heads. More than 100 bald eagles inhabit the river corridor in winter. Also keep an eye out for eagles hunting overhead. Watch, too, for rough-legged and red-tailed hawks, kestrels, merlins, and golden eagles. Winter songbirds in riparian areas include chickadees, juncos, waxwings, and various sparrows. Most land is private, so stay on the roadway. View very carefully from the road or by parking well off the pavement and walking out onto bridges to look up and downstream. **Use great caution walking or parking along this busy highway.**

Ownership: PVT (CDOW for information, 970-472-4300)

Size: 45 miles

Closest town: Kersey, Fort Morgan; lodging, restaurants

Directions: *See map this page*

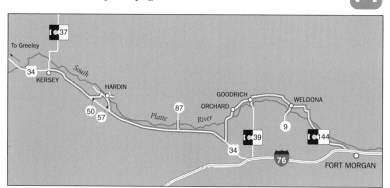

Winter is the time to see bald eagles in Colorado. Watch along larger streams and rivers and the open water below dams.
MACK AND SHARON JOHNSON

Description: Leks, or dancing grounds, are flat, open grassland areas used by successive generations of prairie-chickens during spring courtship. Prairie grassland is essential to provide cover and forage for the birds. All the prairie-chicken leks are on private land and can be visited only on private tours. It's possible to drive some county roads north of Wray and watch for birds from the road.

Viewing information: The spring courtship dance of the greater prairie-chicken is a fascinating sight as the males fluff up, strut, spar, erect the feathers on their heads, and emit a "booming" sound from the air sacs on their necks. Greater prairie-chickens were endangered in Colorado but have recovered significantly due in part to cooperative efforts between public agencies and private landowners. They have been removed from the state endangered species list. Viewers should arrive well before dawn and remain in vehicles. Primary viewing mid-March to May at dawn and dusk. Guided viewing tours offered weekends in March and April, sponsored by CDOW, East Yuma County Historical Society, Wray Museum and Wray Chamber of Commerce. Online information and bookings at **www.WrayChamber.net**.

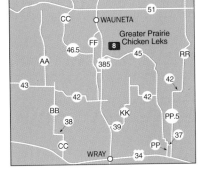

Ownership: PVT
(call Wray Chamber of Commerce for information, 970-332-3484)·

Size: N/A

Closest town: Wray, up to 20 miles; restaurants, lodging

Directions: *See map this page*

Found in grassland country with sandy soils, the male greater prairie-chicken boasts a distinctive orange air sac. Its cousin, the lesser prairie-chicken, is characterized by a pink air sac. W. PERRY CONWAY

9. BONNY LAKE STATE PARK/SOUTH REPUBLICAN STATE WILDLIFE AREA

Description: A large complex of habitats including plains grassland, reservoir, agricultural land, and excellent cottonwood/willow lowland riparian areas around the 1,900-acre reservoir and along the river. Some remnants of native prairie exist. www.parks.state.co.us • www.wildlife.state.co.us

Viewing information: Songbirds in woodlands near Wagonwheel Campground. Look for strutting wild turkeys in spring at Foster Grove Campground. White pelicans and wading birds at water's edge. Good opportunity to see wood ducks with young in spring and summer. Watch for turkey vultures, beaver, and muskrat on the west end. Wintering bald eagles on the lake and good winter waterfowl viewing. Migrant snow geese visible mid-October to mid-November and in March; sandhill cranes in October at the southwest corner of the lake. Also loons, egrets, herons, white-faced ibis, black terns, tundra swans, white-fronted and snow geese, woodpeckers, eastern bluebirds, orchard orioles, and eastern screech owls. White-tailed and mule deer seen year-round in corn and hay fields.

Ownership: CDOW, PVT, State Parks (970-354-7306)

Size: 13,140 acres

Closest town: Idalia, 7 miles; restaurants, lodging

Directions: *See map this page*

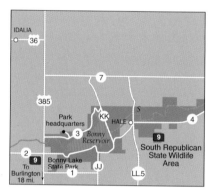

A watery oasis on eastern Colorado's dry plains, Bonny Reservoir is part of an extensive system of riparian and prairie habitats set in a vast agricultural region.
D. ROBERT FRANZ

Description: Small prairie reservoir surrounded by agricultural land. Reservoir water level fluctuates. Below the dam is a cattail wetland, with some willow and cottonwood. www.wildlife.state.co.us

Viewing information: Watch for pheasants and wild turkeys in upland areas. Usually good opportunity to see waterfowl on the reservoir: mallards, pintails, coots, canvasbacks, wigeons, Canada and occasional snow geese. Concentrations of up to 130 white pelicans can be seen in spring and fall. In low water years, there may be some shorebirds. Great blue herons are frequently seen. Golden eagles, Swainson's and red-tailed hawks in migration. Songbirds in riparian areas. Good viewing of grassland songbirds—meadowlarks, lark buntings—and riparian songbirds among cottonwoods and willows in spring and summer. Watch for nighthawks and turkey vultures. White-tailed and mule deer fairly common.

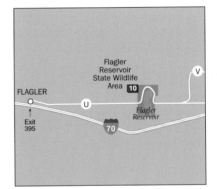

Ownership: CDOW (719-227-5200)

Size: 400 acres

Closest town: Flagler, 3.75 miles

Directions: *See map this page*

Pintails are distinguished by long, pointed tails and prominent white stripes extending up both sides of their heads. The birds are common spring and fall migrants through Colorado.

D. ROBERT FRANZ

Description: This 8-acre wetland was created to replace other wetlands altered or destroyed by highway construction. Water depth varies from 6 inches to 4 feet, creating marshes and small ponds. Nearly 16,000 wetland plants were hand-planted here in 1997, including bulrushes, sedges, cordgrass, and pond-weed; and shrubs such as willows, chokecherry, plum, currant, snowberry, wild rose, three-leaf sumac, and four-wing saltbush.

Viewing information: Excellent for waterfowl including mallards; pintails; shovelers; wigeons; blue-winged, green-winged, and cinnamon teal; gadwalls; redheads; wood ducks. Good for wading and shorebirds, particularly during migration. White-faced ibis, avocets, great blue herons, killdeer, sandpipers; also eared grebes, double-crested cormorants, coots, kingfishers, red-winged and yellow-headed blackbirds. One of the few places in the state to see great-tailed grackles, a species that is expanding its range into Colorado. **Visitors must stay on the trail.**

Ownership: Town of Limon (719-775-2346)

Size: 14 acres

Closest town: Limon, in town; lodging, restaurants

Directions: See map this page

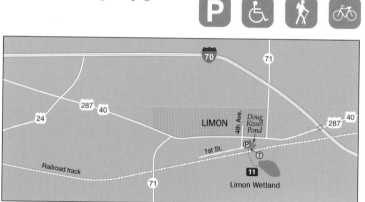

Yellow-headed blackbirds are found in marshes and ponds up to about 8,000 feet in elevation. They prefer to nest over deeper water than their more common cousin, the red-winged blackbird.
WENDY SHATTIL/BOB ROZINSKI

12. SIMLA PRONGHORN LOOP

Description: This driving loop beginning and ending at Simla passes through rolling shortgrass prairie and agricultural land typified by blue grama, buffalo grass, yucca, sagebrush, rabbitbrush, and other shrubs and flowering plants.

Viewing information: Very good opportunity for viewing pronghorn year-round, as well as mule deer and white-tailed deer in riparian habitat along waterways. Coyotes may be seen, as can grassland songbirds such as meadowlarks and horned larks. Watch for raptors soaring or perched on poles and in trees—Swainson's hawks in summer, rough-legged hawks in winter, red-tailed hawks year-round. Property is private, so view only from the road. **When stopping, pull carefully to the side of the road and watch for traffic.**

Ownership: PVT

Size: 30-mile loop

Closest town: Simla; lodging, restaurants

Directions: See map this page

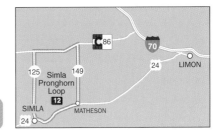

13. KINNEY LAKE STATE WILDLIFE AREA

Description: Rolling terrain, primarily shortgrass prairie. Several small spring-fed ponds with scattered stands of cottonwoods. Two low-lying cottonwood/willow riparian areas. **www.wildlife.state.co.us**

Viewing information: Good viewing of grassland species. Watch for jackrabbits, cottontails, coyotes, numerous muskrats on the ponds, pronghorn, and mule and white-tailed deer. Some resident mallards, occasional other ducks in migration. Grassland songbirds include meadowlarks, horned larks, and lark buntings. Numerous mourning doves in wooded areas and red-winged blackbirds in marshy spots. Raptors include Swainson's and rough-legged hawks, and northern harriers.

Ownership: CDOW (719-227-5200)

Size: 2,240 acres

Closest town: Hugo, 13.5 miles; restaurants, lodging

Directions: See map this page

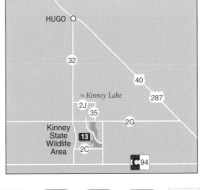

33

Description: Three miles of cottonwood and willow riparian woodlands and wetlands along the floodplain of Fountain Creek. Adjacent meadows, marshes, and ponds support five distinct biological communities. Surface water and lush adjacent wetland vegetation create a natural corridor for migrating wildlife. www.adm.elpaso.co.com/parks

Viewing Information: Active great blue heron nesting colony in the cottonwood trees adjacent to the creek has hosted 82 nests in past years. Excellent birding, especially for migrant songbirds utilizing the riparian habitat and waterbirds on the creek and ponds. The birdlist contains 257 species. Good for reptiles including snapping, painted and western box turtles, pond sliders, six-lined racerunners, bullsnakes, garter snakes. Mammals include black-tailed prairie dogs, fox squirrels, beavers, muskrats, coyotes, red foxes, raccoons, striped skunks, bobcats, white-tailed deer. The nature center offers on-site nature interpreters, natural history information and public programs.

Ownership: El Paso County Parks, (Nature center, 719-520-6745)

Size: 352 acres

Closest Town: Fountain, adjacent; restaurants, lodging

Directions: See map this page

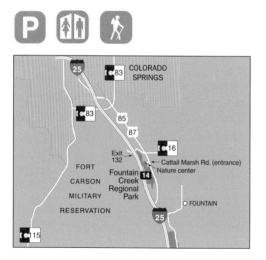

Description: Three very large sites—two working ranches and a U.S. Army installation—comprise a contiguous parcel of prairie and ranchland. The 23,000-acre **Pueblo Chemical Depot** is shortgrass prairie of native grasses, rabbitbrush, yucca, and cholla with some areas of greasewood and sand sage. Chico Creek is bordered by riparian woodlands of cottonwoods, and willows. Lynda Ann Reservoir is a 17-acre lake. The 42,000-acre **Bohart Ranch** is owned by the State Land Board and managed by The Nature Conservancy. The site is sand sage prairie of sand sagebrush and sand bluestem, with areas of shortgrass prairie of blue grama and needle-and-thread grass. Black Squirrel Creek is in the northwest corner. The 86,000-acre **Chico Basin Ranch** is owned by the State Land Board and operated as a working cattle ranch. For hiking, birding, nature interpretation, hunting, fishing, dude ranch vacations, and other visitor opportunities, visit www.ChicoBasinRanch.com.

Viewing information: All three sites are home to typical eastern plains wildlife including pronghorn, coyotes, swift foxes, badgers, and grassland birds including meadowlarks, lark buntings, scaled quail, Cassin's and grasshopper sparrows, mountain plovers, burrowing owls. Very good for raptors, with bald eagles and rough-legged hawks in winter. Some waterfowl and marsh and wading birds can be seen at wetlands and waterways. Reptiles and amphibians include western rattlesnakes, bullsnakes, coachwhips, fence lizards, box turtles, checkered whiptails, lesser earless lizards, bullfrogs, leopard frogs, and tiger salamanders. Many roads are unimproved and difficult to travel in wet weather. Public visitation is limited and requires advance notice. The Nature Conservancy, (303-444-2950) offers some viewing opportunities, by reservation, at Bohart Ranch. Access to the Pueblo Chemical Depot is limited. Contact Public Affairs, (719-549-4135) for current information or to arrange a visit. To find out about current activities or arrange a visit to Chico Basin Ranch, call 719-683-7960.

Ownership: U.S. Army (Pueblo Chemical Depot, 719-549-4135), State Land Board

Size: 151,000 acres

Closest town: Pueblo, 13 miles; Hanover, 2 miles; Ellicott, 8 miles; lodging, restaurants

Directions: See map this page

Description: Located just north of the Arkansas River, the wildlife area is a mix of woodlands (Russian olive, cottonwood, box elder) and shrubs with open areas of grasses, forbs, and weedy species. Thick woodlands on nearby hillsides, wet bottomlands along the Arkansas River and small ponds. The Wildlife Area consists of three tracts—Rocky Ford, McClelland and Melon Valley—along the Arkansas River. **www.wildlife.state.co.us**

Viewing information: Good for migrating birds and nesting eastern songbirds, including orchard oriole, northern waterthrush, northern bobwhite, red-headed woodpecker, yellow-breasted chat. High concentration of nesting blue grosbeaks. The thick hillside woodlands can be alive with migrants in spring. Look for Bohemian and cedar waxwings; spotted towhee; swamp, white-throated, and Harris's sparrows in winter. Check pond near parking lot for green heron. Nearby **Holbrook Reservoir** and **Lake Cheraw** good for shorebirds, gulls, terns, and waterfowl, particularly during migration. Highest concentration of black-necked stilts in Colorado. Also snowy plovers, ruddy ducks, eared grebes, redheads.

Ownership: CDOW (719-336-6600)

Size: 550 acres

Closest town: Rocky Ford, 2 miles; lodging, restaurants

Directions: See map this page

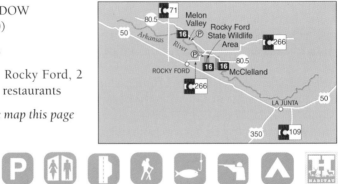

Two nicknames for the male ruddy duck, shown here in breeding plumage, are "stiff-tail" and "blue-bill." Watch for its bobbing and spluttering courtship behavior in winter and early spring. CATHY AND GORDON ILLG

EASTERN PLAINS

Description: Shortgrass prairie surrounds the lake, with stands of tamarisk and cottonwood on the north shore. Portions of the area are closed in winter to protect waterfowl, from November 1 through March. The water levels fluctuate in this irrigation reservoir, which affects the amount of wildlife seen year-to-year. www.wildlife.state.co.us

Viewing information: This is a prime prairie birdwatching site with outstanding waterfowl and shorebird viewing. Three to four hundred white pelicans gather here in summer. Endangered least terns nest on an **island which is closed to public access**. Also a nest site for piping plovers, a threatened species. Please respect these rare birds' nesting sensitivity. Thousands of waterfowl use this lake during migration, primarily Canada geese, mallards, pintails, gadwalls, wigeons, and some teal. Snow geese are also seen. Watch for pheasants and scaled quail. Up to 5,000 sandhill cranes stop here during fall migration. Good winter concentrations of bald eagles which roost in the cottonwoods. Occasional golden eagles, and peregrine falcons have been seen here. Excellent chance to see pronghorn on the drive into the area. Watch for mule deer around the lake.

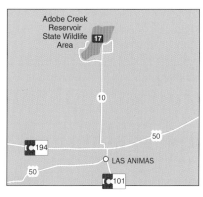

Ownership: CDOW (719-336-6600)

Size: 5,147 acres

Closest town: Las Animas, 13 miles; restaurants, lodging

Directions: See map this page

Snow geese make their fall migrations in large numbers. Their largest concentrations occur at southeast Colorado lakes and reservoirs. Snow geese are easily recognized by their white bodies and black wing tips.
D. ROBERT FRANZ

Description: This state wildlife area encompasses several large, open reservoirs—Neenoshe, Neegronda, Neesopah, and Upper and Lower Queens—surrounded by agricultural fields and shortgrass prairie. Thin bands of cottonwoods grow along high water marks and there are sandy and muddy shores in low-water areas. Water levels fluctuate substantially due to irrigation needs. Bird species vary depending on the water level. Birds can be seen on the water from your vehicle. www.wildlife.state.co.us

Viewing information: Excellent for shore and wading birds in low-water years—phalaropes, avocets, sandpipers, black-necked stilts, and dowitchers. Piping plovers, a threatened species, and endangered least terns have nested here in recent years. Observe the signs denoting sensitive wildlife nesting areas along the beach. Piping plovers nest on the sand so **don't drive vehicles on the beach or allow dogs to chase the birds**. Some snowy plovers and large accumulations of white pelicans. Snow geese numbers impressive in late February and early March in high water years. Masses of migrating sandhill cranes are often seen from the end of February through early April. Variety of dabbling and diving ducks; also western, Clark's, eared, pied-billed, and horned grebes. Occasional longspurs among flocks of horned larks in upland areas in winter and spring. Mud Lake, west of Neenoshe and U.S. Highway 287 at mile marker 100, is very good for water and shorebirds.

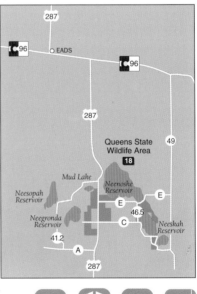

Ownership: PVT, State Parks, BLM, CDOW (719-336-6600)

Size: 4,426 acres

Closest town: Eads, 12.5 miles; restaurants, lodging

Directions: See map this page

Typically seen wading in shallow water, the American avocet is characterized by its thin upturned bill. Its unique black-and-white wings also make it readily identifiable in flight or from a distance.
D. ROBERT FRANZ

EASTERN PLAINS

Description: This municipal park in the city of Lamar is one of the best places in the state to see nesting Mississippi kites.

Viewing information: Mississippi kites arrive in early April, nesting in trees throughout the park. Watch for them flying around the park feeding on flying insects, particularly cicadas. The range of these graceful raptors is expanding. They were first found nesting in Colorado only thirty years ago. Kites leave the area by the end of August.

Ownership: City of Lamar Parks and Recreation Dept. (719-336-2774)

Size: 4 square blocks

Closest town: Lamar; restaurants, lodging

Directions: See map this page

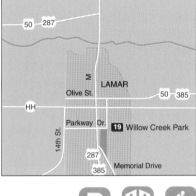

Mississippi kites are an uncommon sight in Colorado. Using their talons, kites catch and eat large insects in the air and grab small rodents and snakes on the ground. CATHY AND GORDON ILLG

Description: Distinct habitats comprise this State Park and adjacent State Wildlife Area. The north shore is rolling shortgrass prairie with bluffs overlooking the lake. The west end, where the Arkansas River feeds the reservoir, is marshy with small ponds. There is a large riparian community along Rule Creek on the south. Access to the water and shoreline is closed during winter migratory waterfowl season on the eastern third of the reservoir. At this time, view with binoculars from pullouts along the road across the dam. Corps of Engineers controls the dam and part of the property. Park visitor center open 9 a.m.–4 p.m. Mon.–Fri. State parks pass required for park entrance, habitat stamp for wildlife area use (can be purchased at visitor center). **www.parks.state.co.us**

Viewing information: The entire north shore is a huge prairie dog colony. Burrowing owls, jackrabbits, bullsnakes, and rattlesnakes inhabit prairie dog burrows. Attracted by the rodents, many predators may be seen in the vicinity including golden eagles, coyotes, badgers, and ferruginous, Swainson's, and red-tailed hawks. Lots of turkey vultures visible early April through late September. From December to February golden eagles and bald eagles use the area. Lots of waterfowl use the lake: wintering snow and Canada geese and mallards, nesting wood ducks, and white pelicans in summer. Good viewing of shorebirds, including piping plovers and least terns. Numerous songbirds are found in the cottonwood stands; active beaver ponds on the west side. Watch for high concentrations of wildlife—songbirds, shorebirds, white pelicans, pheasant, bobwhite and scaled quail, wild turkeys, and deer—in a two-mile section along Rule Creek. Lots of coyotes—watch for them on the ice in winter. To learn about any unusual birds in the area, contact Corps of Engineers, 719-336-3476.

Ownership: Colorado State Parks (719-829-1801), CDOW, Corps of Engineers

Size: 22,000 acres

Closest town:
Las Animas, 5 miles;
 restaurants, lodging

Directions: *See map opposite page*

Black-tailed prairie dogs live in large colonies, or towns, on Colorado's eastern plains. Prairie dog towns are a complex series of interconnected tunnels with more than one entrance.
MICHAEL S. SAMPLE

Description: An area of sagebrush-covered sandhills, interspersed with grasslands. The Purgatoire River runs through the state wildlife area. Several seasonal canals and ponds result in marshy areas. Cottonwood riparian communities along the river, with scattered tamarisk and Russian olive. **www.wildlife.state.co.us**

Viewing information: Watch for beaver sign around ponds; beavers may be seen at dusk and dawn. Good waterfowl viewing year round. Mallards and wood ducks nesting; other ducks include pintails, gadwalls, wigeons, three teal species, and an occasional canvasback. Raptor viewing is especially good in winter for red-tailed, Swainson's, rough-legged, and ferruginous hawks; northern harriers; kestrels; and occasional bald and golden eagles. Great blue herons use the river and ponds, and sandhill cranes fly over during migration. Watch for wild turkeys, pheasants, and bobwhite and scaled quail. Numerous songbirds, especially grassland species such as meadowlarks and lark buntings. Mammals include deer, red foxes, coyotes, and fox squirrels. You may see sign of weasels, bobcats, and raccoons. There is a two-track road but no established hiking trail.

Ownership: CDOW (719-336-6600)

Size: 950 acres

Closest town: Las Animas, 3.5 miles; restaurants, lodging

Directions: See map below

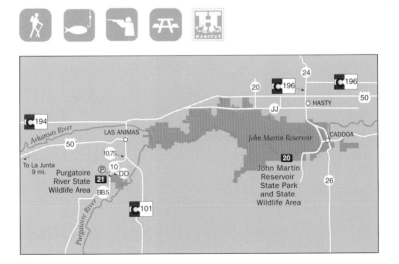

Description: Uplands of shortgrass prairie with juniper woodlands. Two main rocky, steep-walled canyons cut through the area. The canyons are dotted with junipers; a few cottonwoods are scattered along the river tributaries. Both rims of the Apishapa River Canyon are accessible by vehicle, but roads may not be passable in wet weather. **Four-wheel-drive vehicles recommended in bad weather.** Good signs allow access from Highways 10 or 350. www.wildlife.state.co.us

Viewing information: Bighorn sheep inhabit the canyons; binoculars or spotting scopes are needed for good viewing. Watch for pronghorn, mule deer, and coyotes in grassland areas. Meadowlarks and other grassland songbirds common. Scaled quail and mourning doves are numerous, with some wild turkeys. Reptiles include bullsnakes, rattlesnakes, and short-horned and fence lizards. Watch for red-tailed and Swainson's hawks and golden eagles soaring on the thermals.

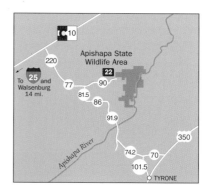

Ownership: CDOW (719-561-5300)

Size: 7,935 acres

Closest town: Walsenburg, 32.5 miles; restaurants, lodging

Directions: *See map this page*

Extremely adaptable, coyotes thrive in a wide range of environments, both urban and wild. These social animals communicate with howls, yips, and barks.
D. ROBERT FRANZ

Description: The canyon is an area of mixed habitats: shortgrass prairie with scattered piñon-juniper woodlands, limestone breaks, red sandstone cliffs, cottonwood riparian zones, some aspen, a basalt ridge along the south, and a series of side canyons along the Purgatoire River. **Call ahead to ensure access as there is no drop-in visitation.** Access is restricted during training activities, particularly in summer. You must first stop at the headquarters office forty-one miles northeast of Trinidad on U.S. 350 to get a pass and area map. There is a $20 annual fee.

Viewing information: Great place to see pronghorn—a herd of about 1,000 live on the Piñon Canyon Military Reservation—as well as 400 to 500 mule deer. Excellent raptor viewing—golden eagles; Swainson's, ferruginous, and red-tailed hawks; and prairie falcons all nest here. Watch also for northern harriers and turkey vultures. Songbirds are common in the grassland riparian areas. Wild turkeys and scaled quail may be seen. Carnivores include coyotes, foxes, and badgers. Beavers along the river; prairie dogs and rabbits in upland areas.

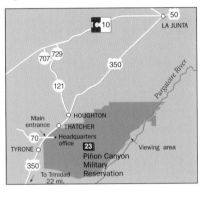

Ownership: U.S. Army (719-524-0123)

Size: 236,000 acres

Closest town: Trinidad, 30 miles; restaurants, lodging

Directions: See map this page

The grumpy badger's powerful front legs enable this expert excavator to dig out its next meal. Badgers live in open terrain throughout Colorado, especially near colonies of ground-dwelling rodents.
WENDY SHATTIL/
BOB ROZINSKI

43

Description: A rocky canyon along the flowing Purgatoire River carved into the open terrain of the shortgrass prairie of southeastern Colorado. Steep descent from the trailhead into the canyon through piñon-juniper habitat and rock formations. The river corridor is a mix of grasslands, cottonwood riparian habitat, pools, and rock faces. More than 1,300 dinosaur footprints cover 700 feet of prehistoric mudflats. Numerous archaeological sites. **www.fs.fed.us**

Viewing information: Abundant variety of wildlife, some of it surprising for southeastern Colorado. Bighorn sheep inhabit the southern end of the canyon. Mule and white-tailed deer, coyotes, badgers, thirteen-lined and spotted ground squirrels. Many reptiles including collared and fence lizards; checkered whiptails; bull, garter, and rattlesnakes. Snapping and soft-shelled turtles in the river. Great variety of birds, particularly during migration—flycatchers, warblers, blue grosbeaks, tanagers, hummingbirds, lazuli buntings, Bullock's and orchard orioles, mockingbirds. Kestrels, turkeys, red-tailed hawks, prairie falcons, scrub jays, golden eagles, great horned and long-eared owls year-round. Good chance to see southwestern species such as roadrunners, scaled quail, brown thrashers, canyon towhees. Watch for the mud nest colonies of cliff swallows beneath rock overhangs. **Four-wheel-drive access by guided tour only. Call in advance for road conditions or special area closures.** Spring and fall best times to visit. Shortgrass prairie uplands leading to the canyon rim are home to pronghorn, coyotes, badgers, lark buntings, horned larks, ferruginous hawks, long-billed curlews, mountain plovers. In late summer and early fall watch at dawn and dusk for swift fox.

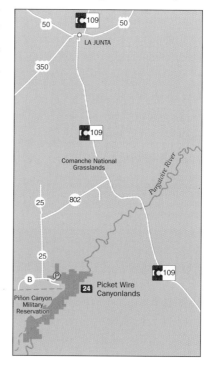

Ownership: USFS (719-384-2181)

Size: 10.5 miles round trip

Closest town: La Junta, 30 miles; lodging, restaurants

Directions: *See map this page*

Dinosaur tracks are only one of the surprises of the Picket Wire Canyonlands on the Comanche National Grassland, a "prairie canyon" surrounded by grasslands.
K. MAX CANESTORP

Description: Shortgrass prairie and old agricultural fields surround a reservoir that is sometimes dry. Cottonwood riparian zones above and below the reservoir, expanding into dry lake bed. A spring below the dam feeds a marshy area. The creek leads into a prairie canyon with Native American petroglyphs on the rocky walls. **www.wildlife.state.co.us**

Viewing information: Good site to view white-tailed and mule deer, pronghorn, cottontails, prairie dogs, and other small mammals. Wild turkeys in morning and evening, also pheasants and scaled quail. As many as 200 turkey vultures roost in cottonwoods at the west end of the property. If the wind is right, golden eagles congregate, using thermals off the buttes. Good fall hawk migration site, with groups, called "kettles," of up to 100 Swainson's hawks. In spring the area below the dam is very good for marsh birds and riparian songbirds—warblers, indigo buntings, blue grosbeaks, brown thrashers, and Bullock's orioles. Good spot for plains, spadefoot, and red-spotted toads; painted and box turtles; collared and fence lizards; and various snakes.

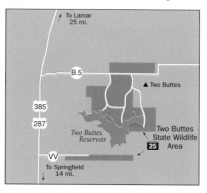

Ownership: CDOW (719-336-6600)

Size: 4,962 acres

Closest town: Springfield, 21 miles; restaurants, lodging

Directions: *See map this page*

Map for Sites 26 and 27

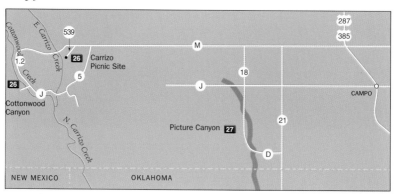

26. CARRIZO PICNIC SITE/COTTONWOOD CANYON

Description: Carrizo and Cottonwood canyons, which are within the Comanche National Grassland, are prairie canyons surrounded by sagebrush uplands dotted with piñon pine and juniper. Rocky terrain on canyon tops with cottonwood riparian areas at the bottom. Access Carrizo Canyon at the picnic site and walk into the canyon. Brands hanging from a cable denote the start of private property. A county road winds through Cottonwood Canyon, but adjacent lands are private. **www.fs.fed.us**

Viewing information: Excellent spring birding for eastern phoebes, wild turkeys, roadrunners, scaled quail, pinyon jays, kingbirds, cliff swallows, mockingbirds, nighthawks, woodpeckers, and hummingbirds. Also Bewick's, rock, and canyon wrens. Turkey vultures common. Excellent raptor site, including nesting hawks, golden eagles, and falcons. Burrowing owls in upland areas. Various toads and frogs around streamside pools. Watch for collared, fence, and western horned lizards. Coachwhips, western hognose snakes, western rattlesnakes, and bullsnakes also common. A herd of bighorn sheep inhabits Cottonwood Canyon, with best viewing late fall and winter. Tarantulas highly visible migrating in fall.

Ownership: PVT, USFS (719-523-6591)

Size: 1,320 acres

Closest town: Campo, 24 miles

Directions: See map opposite page

27. PICTURE CANYON

Description: Part of the Comanche National Grassland, Picture Canyon is named for the Native American pictographs and petroglyphs on its walls. An open, sloping canyon with shortgrass prairie and shrublands on top. Take a 1.5-mile drive into the canyon, accessible by car in dry weather, then a 0.5-mile walk into the rock art area. **www.fs.fed.us**

Viewing information: Excellent site for semi-desert grassland birds. Golden eagles nest here. Other raptors including prairie falcons, kestrels, turkey vultures, and a variety of hawks. Deer, bats, rabbits, and many small mammals. Rattlesnakes are seen, as well as painted and box turtles.

Ownership: USFS (719-523-6591)

Size: 1.5-mile drive, 0.5-mile walk

Closest town: Campo, 15 miles

Directions: See map opposite page

Description: The ancestral lek, or booming ground, is an open area on the shortgrass prairie of the Comanche National Grassland. The best time for viewing is from about one half hour before sunrise until about 9 A.M. Dancing occurs from early March through mid-May, with peak activity in April when the hens arrive. Arrive at the lek well before dawn. If the blind is unavailable, remain in your car to avoid flushing the birds. The birds also display in the evening, but not as dramatically. Binoculars or spotting scopes are recommended. Pronghorn can also be seen in the area. **www.fs.fed.us**

Viewing information: The males' courtship display, meant to attract females, involves bowing, drooping the wings, raising the antennae-like feathers on the head, drumming the feet, pirouetting, and sparring with rival males. The "booming" is made when the birds expel air from brightly colored air sacs on their throats. **Reservations are needed for the viewing blind**.

Ownership: USFS (719-523-6591)

Size: N/A

Closest town: Campo, 13.75 miles

Directions: See map this page

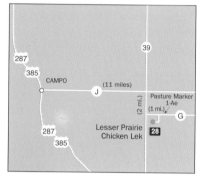

Arrive before daybreak to see the dance of the lesser prairie-chickens. These rarely seen birds return to the lek each spring to take part in this fascinating mating spectacle.
JUDD COONEY

Front Range

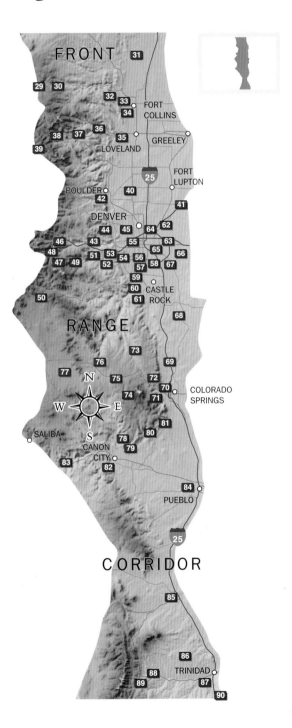

The burgeoning corridor along the Front Range, where the High Plains meet the Rocky Mountains, is home to a surprising abundance and variety of wildlife. Animals of the prairie and foothills inhabit undeveloped areas.

Species that adapt well to life around people roam suburban parks and gardens. Eastern species like white-tailed deer, fox squirrels, and bluejays have migrated west with the planting of trees on the plains.

29. LARAMIE RIVER ROAD

Description: A scenic drive with the mountains of the Rawah Wilderness rising to the west of the river. Primarily dirt road through coniferous woodlands with some stands of aspen. Meadows and willow riparian areas along the river. The road may be closed by snow. **www.fs.fed.us**

Viewing information: Good chance to see moose in willow bottoms, with best viewing where the road is elevated above the river. Golden eagles are visible soaring above ledges. You may see goshawks along the road. Coniferous forest songbirds include gray and Steller's jays, western tanagers, crossbills, and grosbeaks. McGillivray's, Wilson's, and yellow warblers nest in the willows. Marmots inhabit rock outcroppings to the west. Pronghorn and elk may also be seen.

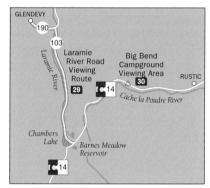

Ownership: PVT, USFS
(970-498-2770)

Size: 15-mile drive

Closest town: Rustic, 20 miles

Directions: *See map this page*

30. BIG BEND CAMPGROUND

Description: Steep, south-facing slope on the north side of the Poudre Canyon. Bitterbrush and sagebrush uplands with scattered Douglas-fir, ponderosa pine, and junipers. Prescribed burns have reduced shrubs and promoted the growth of grass and forbs. For additional information, stop at the Arrowhead Visitor Center (open summer only), three miles west of Rustic on Hwy. 14 and seven miles east of the campground. **www.fs.fed.us**

Viewing information: Excellent bighorn sheep viewing along rocky slopes on the north side of the highway, across the road from the viewing station. Bighorn sheep are sometimes found right on the road. Stay within the viewing site to avoid disturbing the animals. Fee for camping.

Ownership: USFS (970-498-2770)

Size: 10 acres

Closest town: Rustic, 9 miles; restaurants, lodging

Directions: *See map above*

Description: Shortgrass prairie surrounds Hamilton Reservoir, with the Rawhide Energy Station power plant on the north side. Visitors must make advance arrangements for visitation. Viewing is only from the parking lot and from the viewing area on the south shore. **Please stay off the dam.** A visitor's overlook is usually open 7 days a week sunrise to sundown. Check the website or signs at entrance for changes to this schedule. **www.PRPA.org**

Viewing information: Excellent site to view waterfowl and waterbirds October through March. A variety of gulls and ducks sometimes includes oldsquaws; surf and white-winged scoters; Barrow's and common goldeneyes; and common and hooded mergansers. Loons can be seen here; western and Clark's grebes visible May through September. Watch for bald eagles November through February, golden eagles year-round, and ospreys and peregrine falcons during spring and fall migration. Best raptor site is west of the viewing area, where they roost on fence posts and power poles. Merlins can be seen December through March on fences and phone lines along the road into the parking area. When water level is low, beach flats attract a variety of shorebirds. There is a small herd of bison on the grounds.

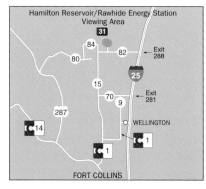

Ownership: Platte River Power Authority (970-226-4000)

Size: 500 acres

Closest town: Wellington, 17.5 miles; restaurants, lodging

Directions: *See map this page*

Eared grebes build nests on shallow ponds and marshes. One of five grebe species that migrate through Hamilton Reservoir, the eared grebe nests in colonies at several sites around the state.

SHERM SPOELSTRA

FRONT RANGE

Description: With elevations ranging from 5,500 to 6,780 feet, this park lies in a transition zone between plains and foothills. This mix of ecosystems—grasslands, foothills, shrublands, riparian areas typified by cottonwood, willow, chokecherry and wild plum, and mountain forest dominated by ponderosa pine, with Douglas-fir and some aspen on cooler slopes—supports a broad diversity of wildlife. www.parks.state.co.us

Viewing information: Mule deer are abundant year-round and often visible browsing among the mountain-mahogany. Cottontails, badgers, snakes, and various rodents inhabit grasslands. Watch for porcupines and Abert's squirrels in pine forests. Though rarely seen, mountain lions and black bears inhabit the park. Common birds include towhees, lazuli buntings, various hawks, goldfinches, vireos, solitaires, orioles, Steller's jays, chickadees, nuthatches, grosbeaks, swallows, nighthawks, wild turkeys, hummingbirds. Take advantage of the visitor center, Watchable Wildlife kiosk, self-guided nature trail, and bird list. Interpretive programs available in summer on request. Backcountry camping only. Hiking trails from the park lead to the adjacent **Horsetooth Reservoir** which supports a variety of migratory waterfowl, shorebirds, raptors, and songbirds. Look for golden and bald eagles, great horned owls, red-tailed and ferruginous hawks. Peregrine falcons use the steep cliffs. Listen for the songs of canyon wrens. Mammal species are the same here as at Lory State Park.

Ownership: State Parks
(970-493-1623)

Size: 2,400 acres

Closest town: Bellvue, 3 miles; restaurants

Directions: *See map this page*

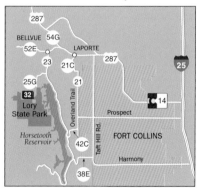

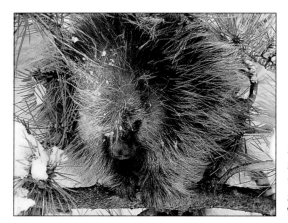

During the day, you may spot nocturnal porcupines by watching for a large, dark shape in the fork of a tree.
WENDY SHATTIL/BOB ROZINSKI

Description: Excellent cottonwood/willow riparian corridor through an urban area. The site encompasses 200 acres of river bottomland and wetlands. A paved trail parallels the Poudre River through Fort Collins, traversing residential, gravel mining, and industrial areas. Numerous public access points. The Colorado State University Environmental Learning Center has two miles of unpaved nature trails open from dawn to dusk seven days a week. The visitor center features interpretive information and displays, and a raptor rehabilitation program. Educational programs help promote environmental stewardship. Call for hours of operation. **www.warnercnr.colostate.edu/elc**

Viewing information: Outstanding opportunity to view wildlife in an urban environment. Active red fox dens, beavers, mule and white-tailed deer, raccoons, fox squirrels, muskrats, and ground squirrels. As many as 206 bird species have been recorded. Excellent for riparian birds in spring and summer. Great waterfowl and waterbird viewing along the river includes Canada geese, a variety of ducks, great blue herons, cormorants, and numerous shorebirds.

Ownership: City of Fort Collins/CSU Environmental Learning Center (970-491-1661)

Size: 8.2 miles, one way

Closest town: Fort Collins, in town

Directions: *See map this page*

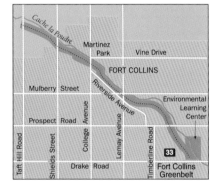

FRONT RANGE

A familiar masked mammal in both urban and rural locales, the raccoon leaves hand-like tracks along wet shorelines.
DENNIS HENRY

34. CATHY FROMME PRAIRIE NATURAL AREA

Description: Rolling terrain dominated by a fairly intact remnant shortgrass prairie. Three tributaries of Fossil Creek, irrigation ditches, and more than 75 acres of wetlands including wet meadows, marshes, and riparian woodlands with exotic trees. The site is classified as a sensitive natural area for its flora and fauna as well as unique and fragile rock outcrops and fossil deposits. www.co.larimer.co.us/parks

Viewing information: Eighty-eight species of birds, mammals, reptiles, and amphibians have been documented on the site. Prairie dog colonies attract abundant raptors, particularly in winter. The raptor observation building has an open blind with interpretive exhibits and excellent raptor viewing. Grassland songbirds, possible nesting burrowing owls. The pond attracts migrant waterfowl, shorebirds, herons. One-and-a-half-mile paved trail.

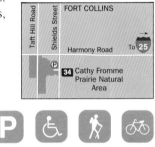

Ownership: City of Fort Collins (970-224-6118 or 970-221-6600)

Size: 1,003 acres

Closest town: Fort Collins, in town; restaurants, lodging

Directions: *See map this page*

35. PINEWOOD, FLATIRON, AND CARTER RESERVOIRS

Description: Three reservoirs set in the foothills of the Front Range. Carter Lake (1,144 surface acres) has a small wetland below Dam No. 2. There is limited riparian habitat along a drainage canal in the northern portion of Pinewood Reservoir (100 surface acres). Flatiron is the smallest lake, with 47 surface acres. A total of 1,200 acres of land around the lakes is open to public recreation. www.co.larimer.co.us/parks

Viewing information: Migratory waterfowl make use of the reservoirs. Canada geese are dominant year-round. Watch for grassland birds year-round; songbirds in migration. Raptors include bald eagles (winter), hawks, and great horned owls. Mammals include mountain lions, bobcats, and black bears. Interpretive exhibits, publications, and a self-guided nature trail along an artificially created wetland are being developed.

Ownership: BOR, Larimer County Parks and Open Lands Department (970-679-4570)

Size: 2,491 acres

Closest town: Loveland, 8 miles

Directions: *See map opposite page*

36. BIG THOMPSON CANYON

Description: This auto tour along U.S. Highway 34 follows the Big Thompson River through a winding, often steep-sided canyon. Parts of the canyon are quite narrow and steep, with sheer cliff faces, while others are more open with grassy meadows. Mountain mahogany and rocky outcrops characterize south-facing slopes, with coniferous forest of ponderosa pine and Douglas-fir on cooler, north-facing slopes.

Viewing information: Bighorn sheep can be seen on the north side of the canyon, especially in winter, grazing on steep, grassy slopes or rocky outcrops. They are less easy to find in spring and early summer when ewes are lambing, or in fall during hunting season. Look for mule deer year-round. Elk may also be seen. Watch for golden eagles soaring above the canyon. Dippers are fairly common along the river. Coyotes may be glimpsed in open areas. Most land is private, so view carefully from the edge of the highway. The road is very winding and oncoming traffic is often obscured, so be very careful. Pull completely off the road, watching for oncoming traffic. A few trailheads access national forest, and the Viestenz-Smith Mountain Park offers picnicking along the river. There are three interpretive signs about bighorn sheep at pullouts.

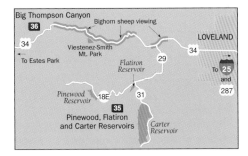

Ownership: CDOT, PVT

Size: 26-mile drive

Closest town: Loveland, 10 miles

Directions: *See map this page*

Spongy pads on the hoofs of bighorn sheep aid them in clinging to sheer cliffs. Scan such cliffs carefully to spot these well-camouflaged animals.
LEE KLINE

Description: The Estes Valley, containing the town of Estes Park, is a mix of highly developed commercial and residential land, paved roads and highways, open space of grasslands and mountain woodlands, Big Thompson River, and Lake Estes reservoir. Dramatic mountain peaks, including 14,255-foot-high Longs Peak, ring the valley. Lake Estes is circled by a 4-mile concrete walking trail. A four-and-a-half-acre bird sanctuary lies on the west side of the lake.

Viewing information: Check open, grassy areas for elk, which can be seen almost everywhere around the area, even in yards and along streets. Watch for bighorn sheep along Fall River Road between Estes Park and the entrance to Rocky Mountain National Park. Other mammals to watch for include mule deer, coyotes, Wyoming ground squirrels, chipmunks, voles, muskrats, and beavers. Lake Estes offers good waterfowl viewing, particularly in fall and winter. Mallards, cinnamon and blue-winged teal, coots, Canada geese, occasional white pelicans. In winter watch for common and Barrow's goldeneyes, common mergansers, redheads, wigeons, and trumpeter and tundra swans, as well as bald eagles, northern shrikes, Thayer's gulls. In spring and early summer check the bird sanctuary for migrants, including hermit thrushes; gray catbirds; cliff and barn swallows; green-tailed towhees; mountain bluebirds; American redstarts; western tanagers; broad-tailed hummingbirds; mountain chickadees; dippers; Cassin's finches; McGillivray's, Wilson's and orange-crowned warblers; Wilson's snipes; spotted sandpipers; and Franklin's and California gulls. Check power poles for prairie falcons and red-tailed hawks. The lake trail is closed from June 1 to June 15 during elk calving.

Ownership: Estes Valley Recreation and Parks District (970-586-8191), BOR, PVT

Size: 350 acres

Closest town: Estes Park; restaurants, lodging

Directions: *See map this page*

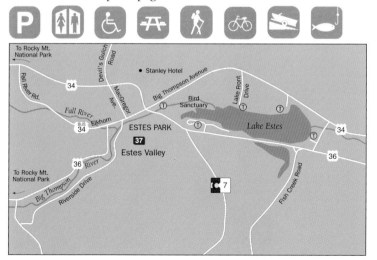

38. ROCKY MOUNTAIN NATIONAL PARK/ MORAINE AND HORSESHOE PARKS

Description: Both of these glacier-carved parks on the eastern side of Rocky Mountain National Park are large mountain meadows of grasses, shrubs, and wildflowers bordered by high-elevation forest of ponderosa pine and Douglas-fir with stands of aspen. The Big Thompson River winds through Moraine Park, creating riverine willow and sedge habitat and marshy wet meadows. Fall River traverses Horseshoe Park. **www.nps.gov**

Viewing information: Both parks are excellent for viewing elk, particularly during the fall rut—September and October—when they may host hundreds of animals. Probably the best site in the state to witness elk bugling, sparring, and mating behavior. Horseshoe Park good for bighorn sheep in fall and winter. Be sure to observe the warning signs against approaching wildlife and the posted seasonal closures: August to mid-October for elk (both parks); May to mid-August for sheep (Horseshoe Park). Paved roads traverse both parks and animals are easily seen from your vehicle, so stay in your car during these times. Coyotes, mule deer, ground squirrels, chipmunks, and cottontails are also commonly seen. Birds are abundant. Watch for dippers along the Big Thompson River. Moraine Park is good for the noisy flight displays of snipes and nighthawks on summer evenings. Interpretive information, guided ranger walks and programs, on-site naturalists (seasonal), a bookstore, exhibits at main visitor center, Moraine Park Museum, Sheep Lakes/Fall River Visitor Center.

Ownership: NPS (970-586-1206)

Size: 3,500 acres

Closest town: Estes Park, 5 miles; lodging, restaurants

Directions: See map next page

Rocky Mountain National Park is an excellent place to view tundra—the land above treeline. Snowmelt from the Never Summer Range, pictured here, feeds the headwaters of the Colorado River.
DAN PEHA

39. ROCKY MOUNTAIN NATIONAL PARK/ KAWUNEECHE VALLEY

Description: This lush valley on the west side of Rocky Mountain National Park is a large area of grassy meadows, high-elevation forests of spruce and fir, willow bogs and marshy wetlands along the Colorado River. Some of the wetlands are 12 to 15 miles long by two to three miles wide. **www.nps.gov**

Viewing information: Excellent place to spot moose feeding in marshy areas. Beavers and occasional river otters can be seen along the river. Watch for elk and mule deer. Birding is very good in marshy areas and surrounding forests, with a great array of forest and wetlands species—warblers, jays, flycatchers, thrushes, woodpeckers, sparrows, grosbeaks, kinglets, hummingbirds. Many small mammals inhabit the various habitats, including pine squirrels, weasels, mink, voles, cottontails, raccoons. The Kawuneeche Visitors Center has maps, bird lists, interpretive information, on-site naturalists, walks, and talks. Some seasonal closures from August to mid-October (as posted) during the elk rut.

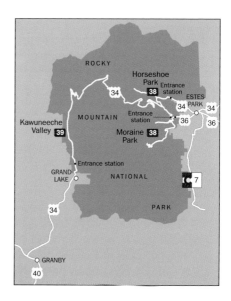

Ownership: NPS (970-627-3471)

Size: 26,000 acres

Closest town: Grand Lake, 5 miles; lodging, restaurants

Directions: *See map this page*

"Scattered bird songs and sunlight shifting through the leaves . . . Captivated by this morning music, I listen intently as the forest comes to life with dawn's first light."—Lisa Brochu

Description: A network of ponds formed from reclaimed gravel pits and surrounding marshes offers excellent habitat for many bird species. Riparian woodlands on the shore and along Boulder Creek, with brushy open areas. www.co.boulder.co.us/openspace

Viewing information: A great many ducks and waterbirds arrive on the ponds in winter and during migration. Shorebirds are attracted to sandbars and mud flats when water levels drop. Tundra swans may be seen in fall. Marsh birds include sora and Virginia rails, Wilson's snipes, white-faced ibis, and American bitterns. Cottonwood Marsh is a good site for herons, grebes, ducks, geese, and yellow-headed and red-winged blackbirds. An abundance of songbirds in riparian areas. Raptors include great horned owls, red-tailed and rough-legged hawks, northern harriers, kestrels, and northern shrikes.

Ownership: City of Boulder Open Space and Mountain Parks (720-564-2000), Boulder County Parks and Open Space (303-678-6200)

Size: 113 acres

Closest town: Boulder, 5.5 miles; restaurants, lodging

Directions: *See map this page*

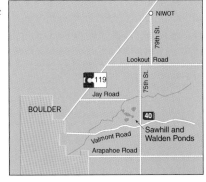

The famed Flatirons form the backdrop for Boulder's Sawhill Ponds. The reclaimed gravel pits boast a diverse population of marsh birds. D. ROBERT FRANZ

FRONT RANGE

Description: A premier birdwatching site. Bird records from Barr Lake date back more than 100 years with over 300 species recorded. Combining three habitats—open-water, shoreline cottonwood/willow woodlands, and grassland—the park is home to a diversity of wildlife. Interpretive programs and displays are offered at the Nature Center. Wooden boardwalks and viewing gazebo are found along the lakeshore. **www.parks.state.co.us**

Viewing information: The lake attracts an array of waterfowl and waterbirds, including geese, white pelicans, grebes, coots, and numerous species of ducks. The shoreline riparian area offers nesting for owls, hawks, songbirds, and wading birds. Great blue herons, black-crowned night-herons, and double-crested cormorants populate a rookery here, but the most famous residents are the pair of nesting bald eagles. Mule deer roam the park. Red foxes den each spring in grassland areas surrounding the lake. Watch for a variety of small mammals—fox squirrels, thirteen-lined ground squirrels, muskrats, pocket gophers, and raccoons. In spring and summer listen for chorus frogs in the ponds along the nature trail. Bullsnakes and several species of turtle also live here.

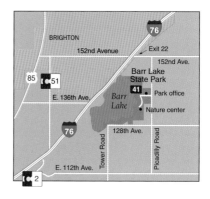

Ownership: State Parks (303-659-6005)

Size: 2,600 acres

Closest town: Brighton, 6.25 miles; restaurants, lodging

Directions: *See map this page*

The thirteen-lined ground squirrel is a common inhabitant of eastern grasslands and mountain parks. It hibernates in winter.
SHERM SPOELSTRA

Description: The south end of this well-marked trail begins along South Boulder Creek in shortgrass prairie intermixed with large patches of tallgrass. Lower elevations have sumac, chokecherry, hawthorn, and juniper. Trail winds through ponderosa pine/Douglas-fir forest with riparian vegetation along numerous canyons. North access in Boulder's Chautauqua Park. www.co.boulder.co.us/openspace

Viewing information: On its course through a transition zone, the trail offers good opportunities to see a diverse mix of plains and mountain species. Excellent raptor watching features golden eagles, great horned owls, prairie and peregrine falcons, goshawks, and Cooper's and red-tailed hawks. Respect closures for raptor nesting. Canyon bottoms are very good for migratory songbirds May through June and August through September. Watch also for Steller's jays, magpies, ravens, and turkey vultures. Deer are visible throughout, but best viewing is from the south trailhead to the National Center for Atmospheric Research (NCAR). Watch for coyotes, and you may see sign of mountain lions year-round and black bears August through November. Small mammals include Abert's and rock squirrels, golden-mantled ground squirrels, chipmunks, and cottontails.

Ownership: City of Boulder Open Space and Mountain Parks (720-564-2000), Boulder County Parks and Open Space (303-678-6200)

Size: 6.7 miles, one way

Closest town: Boulder

Directions: See map this page

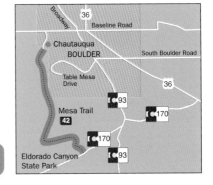

Rock squirrels inhabit rocky country where they can find the vegetation they eat, like this Indian paintbrush. The rock squirrels' loud whistle can help you locate them among the rocks.
DENNIS HENRY

FRONT RANGE

43. GOLDEN GATE CANYON STATE PARK

Description: This foothills park offers varied habitats, including mountain meadows and wooded slopes of mixed conifer and aspen. Elevations range from 7,600 to 10,400 feet. There are 35 miles of hiking trails within the park, and from Panorama Point visitors have scenic views along nearly 75 miles of the Front Range from Mount Evans to Longs Peak. Visitor center with interpretive displays. Brochures available. **www.parks.state.co.us**

Viewing information: Excellent birding site easily accessible from the Denver metro area. Songbirds are abundant in summer. In addition to gray and Steller's jays and Clark's nutcrackers, watch for chickadees, juncos, sapsuckers, western tanagers, grosbeaks, bluebirds, snipes, and tree, barn, and violet-green swallows. Raptors include eagles, prairie falcons, and various owls and hawks. Deer and elk are often seen. Trout viewing pond at the visitor center.

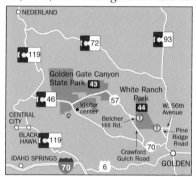

Ownership: State Parks (303-582-3707)

Size: 14,400 acres

Closest town: Golden, 15 miles; restaurants, lodging

Directions: *See map this page*

44. WHITE RANCH PARK

Description: Eighteen miles of hiking and equestrian trails wind through heavily timbered slopes of ponderosa pine and Douglas-fir, with some open areas. Several vantage points offer good vistas to the east of Denver and beyond. An interpretive area has a collection of historical farm equipment. Dogs must be leashed. Camping by permit only. **www.co.jefferson.co.us/openspace**

Viewing information: You're unlikely to see bears, mountain lions, or bobcats, but you may see their tracks and sign. Keep your eyes open for deer, elk, and wild turkeys as well as squirrels and Steller's jays.

Ownership: Jefferson County Open Space (303-271-5925)

Size: 3,040 acres

Closest town: Golden, 3 miles; restaurants, lodging

Directions: *See map above*

Description: Suburban Arvada borders this urban refuge on three sides. The 62.7-acre site, a mix of grasslands and riparian habitats, is dominated by brome grass on uplands intermixed with alfalfa. Native plants such as needle-and-thread grass are found on knolls with rabbitbrush and yucca in drier areas. Irrigation canals, lined with plains cottonwood and Russian olive, cross the refuge. Cattails and willows grow along the three ponds and other moist spots and seeps. Trailheads are on Kipling Street, 80th Avenue just east of the Medical Center, and on 77th Drive. Park at the Medical Center or on 77th Drive off of Kipling. **www.fws.gov/rockymountainarsenal/twoponds**

Viewing information: Ninety-three species of birds have been observed at the refuge, primarily spring through fall, including great blue herons, black-crowned night herons, and various migrating waterfowl and songbirds. Ten nesting species, including Swainson's hawks and western meadowlarks. Mammals include mule deer, raccoons, muskrats, beavers, and red foxes. Watch for leopard frogs and bullfrogs. Painted and snapping turtles may be seen sunning on logs during the warm months. The prairie management area trails are open dawn to dusk seven days a week. The environmental education area is open May through October on Tuesday, Thursday and Saturday to groups of ten or more, by reservation.

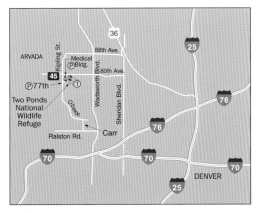

Ownership: USFWS (303-289-0232, ext. 0)

Size: 63 acres

Closest town: Arvada, in town; lodging, restaurants

Directions: See map this page

The hunch-shouldered shapes of black-crowned night herons are a common site along waterways in the Denver metropolitan area.
SHERM SPOELSTRA

FRONT RANGE

46. GEORGETOWN STATE WILDLIFE AREA

Description: Developed interpretive site overlooking nearly year-round bighorn sheep habitat. The viewing area gives excellent views of bighorn sheep habitat across Interstate 70. The tower has coin-operated viewing scopes. The donation helps maintain the site. When you get near, tune your radio to AM 540 for wildlife viewing information. **For safety and to avoid stressing the animals, do not stop on the highway** or use the hillside access road. www.wildlife.state.co.us

Viewing information: Between 300 and 350 bighorn sheep utilize the habitat, often standing very close to the interstate. Bighorn sheep can be seen here nearly every month of the year, but the best viewing is fall, winter, and spring. The facility is hosted by volunteer naturalists on weekends from late November through January, through the rut. Sheep may also be seen near Empire and Grant, though there are no viewing facilities.

Ownership: City of Georgetown (Visitor Center, 303-569-2555), CDOW

Size: 1,000 acres **Closest town:** Georgetown, 1 mile; restaurants, lodging

Directions: *See map this page*

47. GUANELLA PASS

Description: The pass offers access to alpine habitat plus spectacular views of Mt. Evans and Mt. Bierstadt. The route is a scenic byway, but is not maintained in winter. Call for road conditions. Please stay on trails or the road to protect the fragile alpine ecosystem.

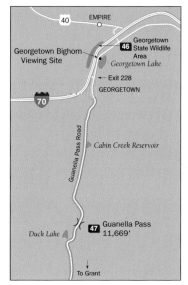

Viewing information: Accessible opportunity to view alpine habitat and wildlife year-round. Possibly the best spot in the United States for viewing white-tailed ptarmigan. Bighorn sheep, mountain goats, and elk are sometimes visible on mountain slopes and in the basin below the summit. Jays, nutcrackers, grosbeaks, and dusky grouse reside in high-elevation forests year-round. Watch also for Abert's squirrels and chickarees. In September raptors and swallows migrating south fly low over the top of the pass.

Ownership: Town of Idaho Springs, PVT, USFS (303 567-2901)

Size: 26 miles   **Closest town:** Georgetown, 9 miles; restaurants, lodging; Grant, 11.25 miles   ***Directions:*** *See map this page*

48. GRAYS AND TORREYS PEAKS

Description: The access road to the trailhead for these twin 14,000-foot-high mountains passes through high-elevation pine forest. **High-clearance vehicles are necessary.** The trail to the summits starts at 11,240 feet and passes through a mosaic of high-elevation forest, mountain meadows, timberline woodlands, extensive willow thickets, and rocky alpine habitat to the summit of Grays Peak at 14,270 feet. The summit of Torreys Peak (14,267 feet) is a half-mile farther. Spectacular views. **www.fs.fed.us**

Viewing information: This is an excellent place for viewing mountain goats, especially in spring, and bighorn sheep (less often seen) as well as alpine-dwellers like marmots, pikas, and pipits. Watch for white-tailed ptarmigan, particularly around the willows. Scan drainages for elk. Mule deer and coyotes are also sometimes seen. A variety of birds and small mammals inhabit the high-elevation forest including chipmunks, golden- and ruby-crowned kinglets, hermit thrushes, and pine grosbeaks. Wilson's warblers and white-crowned sparrows nest in the willows. Many birds move up here later in the summer after young have fledged. Raptors can often be seen at cliffs to the east. The dirt access road is rough and steep and not maintained and can become impassable in wet weather. No motorized vehicles allowed on the trail. Dogs must be on leash.

Ownership: USFS (303-567-2901)

Size: 4 miles, one way

Closest town: Georgetown, 8 miles; lodging, restaurants

Directions: *See map this page*

The neighboring Grays and Torreys Peaks, two of Colorado's "fourteeners," can be climbed together in one day, offering spectacular views and good wildlife viewing.
DANIEL LARSON

Description: The Mount Evans Highway is the highest paved road in the United States. The 14-mile drive from Echo Lake to the summit parking area offers spectacular scenic views as well as dependable wildlife viewing opportunities. Plan on three to four hours to complete the round trip. Good tundra viewing in close proximity to a major metropolitan area. The road ends just before the 14,264-foot summit of Mount Evans. The paved highway is extremely narrow and winding; use caution when stopping to view animals. Road is closed by snow early fall through late spring. Stay on trails around Summit Lake to protect delicate vegetation. **For your safety and the protection of wildlife, do not feed or approach animals.** The USFS visitor center in Idaho Springs has self-guiding interpretive materials. **www.fs.fed.gov**

Viewing information: Beginning at Echo Lake at 10,700 feet, the first few miles of the highway traverse high-elevation forest, home to chickarees, dusky grouse, gray jays, and Clark's nutcrackers. Many songbirds move to this zone in late summer because of abundant food resources. The 1.1-mile trail at the Mount Goliath Natural Area passes through a stand of gnarled bristlecone pine, among the oldest living organisms on earth. Good views from here of elk in meadows and on open slopes. Mountain goats and bighorn sheep often visible on or near the road. Watch rocky slopes above timberline for mountain goats. At Summit Lake a short trail leads along the lake to an overlook with a good chance to see or hear pikas, ptarmigan, marmots, American pipits, and brown-capped rosy finches. Wildflowers are abundant.

Ownership: City of Denver, USFS (303-567-2901)

Size: 14 miles, one way

Closest town: Idaho Springs, 11.25 miles; restaurants, lodging

Directions: *See map this page*

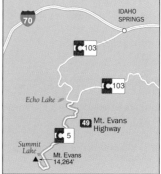

White-tailed ptarmigan escape detection through natural camouflage. Their feathers turn white in winter and a rocklike gray or brown in summer. In winter, ptarmigan burrow into the snow for insulation against the cold nights.

WENDY SHATTIL/BOB ROZINSKI

Description: A variety of habitats characterizes this 10,000-foot pass, the gateway to South Park. High-elevation pond situated within a wet mountain meadow, mountain riparian communities, and aspen and lodgepole pine forests. A sweeping view of South Park to the south. Also an access point with parking lot for the Colorado Trail. **www.fs.fed.us**

Viewing information: The 0.25-mile Waterfowl Watch Trail, which follows a portion of the historic railroad bed, leads to a viewing deck with interpretive panels overlooking the pond. The pond attracts mallards, coots, Canada geese, lesser scaup, gadwalls, ring-necked ducks, green-winged and cinnamon teal, killdeer, spotted sandpipers, Wilson's phalaropes, red-winged blackbirds, and tree swallows. Good spot for migrating waterfowl and songbirds. Check surrounding forests for hermit thrushes, ruby- and golden-crowned kinglets, pine siskins, dusky grouse, red-naped and Williamson's sapsuckers, chickadees, and various flycatchers. Watch for elk in fall and spring migrating to and from wintering grounds in South Park. Other mammals include Wyoming ground squirrels, snowshoe hares, muskrats, mule deer, pine squirrels, chipmunks. Telltale trails of voles crisscross the meadows.

Ownership: USFS (303-275-5610)

Size: 0.25-mile trail

Closest town: Grant, 8 miles; Jefferson, 5.5 miles

Directions: *See map this page*

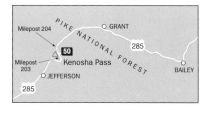

The burnished-copper plumage and brilliant red eye of the male cinnamon teal in breeding plumage make it one of the handsomest of ducks.
WENDY SHATTIL/
BOB ROZINSKI

Description: A variety of mountain habitats in this park: meadows, ponderosa pine and Douglas-fir woodlands, aspen groves, pine forest, and the exposed terrain around the summit of 9,708-foot Bergen Peak. Controlled burns assure the health of the habitat. Numerous marked hiking trails. Good scenic views. Dogs must be leashed. **www.co.jefferson.co.us/openspace**

Viewing information: In the lower-elevation meadows watch for elk, deer, coyotes, Wyoming ground squirrels, and other small mammals. The ponderosa pine forest is home to Abert's squirrels, chipmunks, and other ground squirrels. Ravens are common. Look for red-tailed and Swainson's hawks soaring on thermals over open areas. The park encompasses several wildlife preserves, including the Bergen Peak State Wildlife Area. **Stay on the trail to avoid stressing the animals.** In early summer the meadow wildflowers are outstanding. Interpretive and park information is available at trailhead kiosks, and there is elk viewing information along Colorado Highway 103.

Ownership: CDOW, Denver Mountain Parks, Jefferson County Open Space (303-271-5925)

Size: 3,000 acres

Closest town: Evergreen, 3 miles, restaurants, lodging; Bergen Park, 1 mile

Directions: *See map this page*

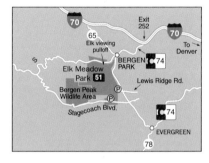

The Abert's squirrel is one of the few Colorado animals associated exclusively with a single plant community. Ponderosa pines provide these "tassel-eared" squirrels with all the essentials—food, shelter, and nest sites. WENDY SHATTIL/BOB ROZINSKI

52. LAIR O' THE BEAR

Description: Mixed community of cottonwood, alder, willow, chokecherry, and box-elder along Bear Creek. Trails enter a narrow canyon with blue spruce and Douglas-fir on north-facing slopes, and an understory of ferns and mosses. South-facing slopes are a mixture of ponderosa pine, juniper, and other shrubs. About 3 miles of trail, including a 0.5-mile self-guided nature trail. Dogs must be leashed. Some trails are for hiking only with no horses or bikes allowed. www.co.jefferson.co.us/openspace

Viewing information: Active beaver colony along the creek. Elk viewing best in fall and winter. Dippers are visible along the creek. Good site for songbirds, including warblers, orioles, magpies, western tanagers, and Steller's jays. Watch for kestrels and woodland hawks.

Ownership: Jefferson County Open Space (303-271-5925)

Size: 319 acres

Closest town: Kittredge, 4 miles

Directions: See map this page

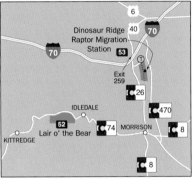

53. DINOSAUR RIDGE RAPTOR MIGRATION STATION

Description: An open site above the town of Morrison atop the Dakota Ridge stretching north and south along the Front Range west of Denver. Beginning at the parking lot at the southeast corner of Interstate 70 and Colorado Highway 26, take the trail to the top of the hogback. The observation site is about a half-hour walk from the parking lot—a steep, 0.25-mile hike. Good views of migrating raptors and the Denver metro area to the east. Volunteers assist visitors March to mid-May. You may also access the trail from the parking area for Matthews/Winters Open Space Park, across Highway 26. www.co.jefferson.co.us/openspace

Viewing information: Migration corridor for a variety of raptors. More than 3,500 birds, representing 17 species, can be seen in an eight-week period in spring. Watch for eagles and hawks. Later in April look for hawks, kestrels, merlins, and falcons. Turkey vultures and ospreys are often visible.

Ownership: Jefferson County Open Space, RMBO, Lookout Mountain Nature Center (720-497-7600)

Size: 0.25-mile, one way

Closest town: Morrison, 4.75 miles; restaurants, lodging

Directions: See map above

Description: Located at the edge of the High Plains where Bear Creek drains out of the foothills, this 2,600-acre park offers a mix of open, rolling grasslands, man-made lakes, riparian habitat, and a golf course. Grassland areas support a variety of native shortgrass prairie vegetation including western wheatgrass, blue grama, yucca, prickly pear and rabbitbrush. Cottonwoodlands along the creek have an understory of shrubs. The golf course is a highly managed habitat: mowed, watered, and fertilized. **www.lakewood.org**

Viewing information: The open water of Bear Creek Lake, created by a dam along Bear Creek, attracts a variety of water birds, particularly in summer, including Canada geese, mallards, shovelers, redheads, canvasbacks, wood ducks, common mergansers, coots, white pelicans, grebes, cormorants, great blue herons. Bald eagles hunt the lake in winter and golden eagles are common year-round. American dippers can be seen along the creek in winter. A variety of small mammals—black-tailed prairie dogs, pocket gophers, cottontails—attract red-tailed, Swainson's, and ferruginous hawks; prairie falcons; and great horned owls, which can be seen almost nightly throughout the year. Various songbirds seen in summer, especially in riparian areas. The bird list contains 114 species. Mule deer inhabit the park and elk are occasionally seen. Other mammals include red foxes, coyotes, raccoons, muskrats, fox squirrels. Bear Creek Lake Park Visitor Center offers interpretive exhibits, on-site naturalists, checklists, and nature walks.

Ownership: City of Lakewood (303-697-6159), Army Corps of Engineers

Size: 2,600 acres

Closest town: Lakewood, in town; restaurants, lodging

Directions: *See map this page*

The northern shoveler's spoon-shaped bill distinguishes it. Watch for a group of shovelers swimming together in a circle, each feeding on bits of food stirred up by the paddling of the others.
ROBERT E. BARBER

Description: A paved trail meanders through an urban greenbelt following Clear Creek. Cottonwood/willow community along the creek borders open meadows, offering excellent edge habitat. Four reservoirs west of the park provide open water year-round for waterfowl viewing. Greenbelt access is from Johnson Park, Anderson Park, Prospect Park, and Youngfield Street between 38th and 44th Avenues.

Viewing information: An important wildlife corridor and outstanding opportunity for urban wildlife viewing. More than 180 bird species have been recorded here. An abundance of songbirds are attracted to the riparian zones along the creek—woodpeckers, warblers, grosbeaks, tanagers, flycatchers, vireos. Year-round waterfowl viewing on open creek and reservoirs. Many wetland birds, Wilson's snipe, sora, and Virginia rails. Watch for dippers along the creek in winter. Mammals include muskrats, red foxes, and raccoons. Beavers reside in the Anderson Park and Johnson Park areas.

Ownership: City of Wheat Ridge (303-205-7552)

Size: 270 acres

Closest town: Wheat Ridge, in town

Directions: *See map this page*

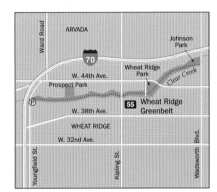

FRONT RANGE

The male western tanager is one of Colorado's most colorful species. Western tanagers migrate through urban habitats along the Front Range en route to their nesting area in coniferous forests.
WENDY SHATTIL/BOB ROZINSKI

Description: Thirty-mile paved bike and walking path of the South Platte River Greenway follows the South Platte River from Chatfield State Park to the river's confluence with Clear Creek. A variety of urban landscapes includes light industrial, residential, open space, and suburban parks. Cottonwood riparian zones along much of the river. Excellent urban wildlife corridor. Sixteen municipal parks are located along the greenway, including South Platte Park in Littleton with the only remaining piece of the South Platte River through Denver that isn't channelized. Much of the river is also boatable by nonmotorized craft. There are numerous trail access points along the route. The Adams County Greenway will soon link Brighton and Barr Lake to the river greenway and link the Clear Creek Trail to Jefferson County's trail system along Clear Creek. It is rural in character, often winding through groves of cottonwoods and past ponds. The trail connects with a nature preserve at the north end of the Adams County Regional Park, near 124th Street. **www.greenwayfoundation.org**

Viewing information: Ducks—including mallards, gadwalls, shovelers, hooded mergansers, and goldeneyes—are visible on the river, especially in winter. Watch for great blue herons, black-crowned night herons, and belted kingfishers at water's edge. Many mammals use this riverine corridor, including beavers, muskrats, red foxes, raccoons, skunks, deer. Numerous songbirds inhabit the cottonwood/ willow woodlands along the river, especially in spring and summer.

Ownership: Multiple counties and municipalities, Greenway Foundation (303-455-7109)

Size: 30 miles, one way

Closest town: Metro Denver; restaurants, lodging

Directions: *See map this page*

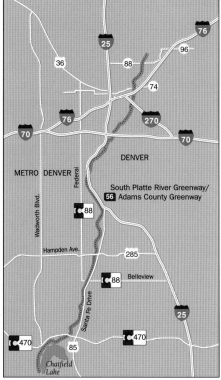

Canada geese flourish in Colorado. Their in-flight V-formations and familiar honking make them especially popular among state wildlife watchers. TOM TIETZ

Description: This natural area along the South Platte River includes more than 85 acres of diverse urban wetlands, a 2.5 mile unchannelized stretch of the South Platte River, and over 235 acres of surface water. The balance of the park is mixed riparian woodland, old fields, and dense shrublands. Vegetation is a mix of remnant native species, weedy exotic plants, and non-native shrubs and trees. www.sspr.org/southsubnew/nature

Viewing information: Winter offers great waterfowl viewing along the South Platte including hooded mergansers, common goldeneyes, wood ducks, pintails, ring-necked ducks, and many other species. Good chance to see bald eagles and nesting great horned owls. Red-tailed and Swainson's hawks (summer). Excellent for migrating birds in spring, with as many as 75 different species sometimes seen in a single day. Fifty-four confirmed nesting species of birds. Spring and summer are good for white-tailed deer. Other mammals include raccoons, skunks, squirrels, coyotes. There are seven to ten active beaver lodges in the park, with best viewing in fall and winter. Seven miles of trails, both hard and natural surface, traverse the park. A viewing blind is located between two lakes in the southern end of the park. The park is open year-round from dawn to dusk. Carson Nature Center is open Tuesday through Friday noon to 4pm, Saturday and Sunday 9:30 a.m. to 4:30 p.m. It offers interpretive exhibits and programs, on-site naturalists, checklists, brochures, maps, and a trailside guide.

Ownership: City of Littleton, South Suburban Park and Recreation District (Carson Nature Center, 303-730-1022)

Size: 659 acres   **Closest town:** Littleton, 3 miles; lodging, restaurants

Directions: See map this page

Description: This historic irrigation canal loops and winds 71 miles through the Denver metropolitan area. Though it holds water only seasonally, much of its route is lined with urban riparian forest, with grassy or shrubby banks. Paved and unpaved trails follow the canal and are accessible at many points. Some good sites for wildlife viewing include: (1) the canal crosses County Line Road near McLellan Reservoir, west of Broadway in Highlands Ranch—walk southeast; (2) DeKoevend Park, on University Boulevard north of the Southglenn Mall in Littleton—walk west along the canal and Big Dry Creek; (3) Horseshoe Park and wetlands, walk two miles north from the parking area on Orchard Road in Greenwood Village; (4) East Quincy Avenue and Dahlia Street in Cherry Hills—walk southeast to a wetlands and open space, or northwest to Three Pond Park; (5) Eisenhower Park between Yale and Hampden, on the east side of Colorado Boulevard in Denver; (6) Expo Park in Aurora between Alameda and Exposition east of Havana—walk north along the canal. www.denverwater.org

Viewing information: Excellent urban wildlife viewing along a historic canal. Watch in the riparian woodlands lining the canal for flickers, chickadees, orioles, song sparrows, kingfishers, woodpeckers, Cooper's and sharp-shinned hawks, great horned owls, and a great variety of songbirds, particularly during migration. Look for beavers and red foxes. Bats are often seen on summer evenings. In ponds along the route or when there is water in the canal, watch for waterfowl and a variety of shorebirds. Keep an eye out for turtles sunning on the banks.

Ownership: Denver Water (Recreation office, 303-628-6526)

Size: 71 miles

Closest town: Denver and surrounding communities; lodging, restaurants

Directions: *See map opposite page*

Description: Located where the prairie meets the foothills, this state park attracts both grassland and mountain wildlife. In spring the landform also funnels migratory birds following the South Platte River west from the Great Plains into a small area as the river enters the narrow confines of Waterton Canyon. Fall migrants follow the Front Range south to this area. Grassland areas surround a 1,150-acre reservoir. Plum and Deer creeks, the South Platte River, and the Highline Canal traverse the park, supporting an extensive cottonwood/willow/box-elder riparian community. Large cattail marsh along Plum Creek. A wetlands area in the southwest corner of the park has an interpretive trail that leads to an observation gazebo. A viewing blind with interpretive signs and viewing scopes at the overlook allows possible viewing of herons passing through or feeding. **www.parks.state.co.us**

Viewing information: Nearly 345 species of birds have been recorded here. A premier spot in Colorado for woodland birds and migrants along the river: house wrens, wood pewees, swallows, vireos, woodpeckers, eight species of swallows, and 32 species of warblers. Good waterfowl viewing on the reservoir in spring and fall. Watch also for red-winged and yellow-headed blackbirds, coots, grebes, loons (in fall), and kingfishers. Great blue herons and double-crested cormorants are highly visible. Occasional migrant osprey. The overlook on the southeast side of the reservoir is a particularly good bird observation point. Lots of beavers and mule deer.

Ownership: State Parks (303-791-7275)

Size: 5,600 acres

Closest town: Littleton, 10 miles; restaurants, lodging

Directions: *See map this page*

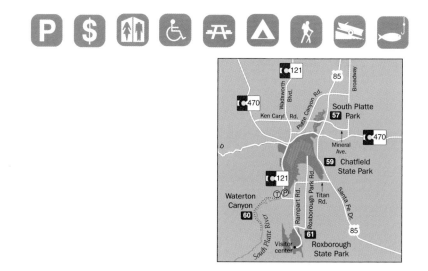

60. WATERTON CANYON

Description: Lower canyon access follows a road along the South Platte River to the beginning of the Colorado Trail. The road was built on the old bed of the Denver, South Park, and Pacific Narrow Gauge Railroad. Very popular for mountain biking. Habitat changes with elevation, from shrublands to Douglas-fir/ponderosa pine. Cottonwoods, willow thickets, and box-elder along the river. The canyon is accessible by foot, horseback, or bike only. **Dogs and motorized vehicles (except official vehicles) are prohibited.** www.denverwater.rog

Viewing information: The cliffs offer good nesting for golden eagles and turkey vultures. Watch for Cooper's and sharp-shinned hawks in higher-elevation coniferous forests. Songbirds in riparian areas. Bighorn sheep sometimes visible near or on the road, but do not approach them. Watch also for mule deer. Good chance to see dippers along the river. Wintering bald eagles patrol the river from a major roosting site at Cheesman Reservoir.

Ownership: USFS (303-275-5610), Denver Water Dept., PVT

Size: 6 miles   **Closest town:** Littleton, 10 miles; restaurants, lodging

Directions: See map opposite page

61. ROXBOROUGH STATE PARK

Description: Characterized by red rock formations, Roxborough is located in a transition zone between plains and foothills. Grasslands and oak brush shrublands mixed with wet meadows; cottonwood/box-elder communities along Little Willow Creek. Ridgetops and slopes of Carpenter Peak feature ponderosa pine/Douglas-fir. Several aspen groves in moist, sheltered areas, well below the species' usual altitude. Excellent geological site. www.parks.state.co.us

Viewing information: Watch for mule deer, elk, coyotes, and many small mammals. You may see signs of bobcat, mountain lion, and bear. Good raptor viewing, including prairie falcons, golden eagles, kestrels, and red-tailed hawks. The park checklist includes over 140 bird species. Reptiles include bullsnakes, rattlesnakes, hognose and garter snakes, box turtles, chorus frogs, fence lizards, and yellow-bellied racers. **No dogs are allowed in the park.**

Ownership: State Parks (303-973-3959)

Size: 3,299 acres

Closest town: Littleton, 13 miles; restaurants, lodging

Directions: See map opposite page

Description: A small portion of the 17,000 acres of the Rocky Mountain Arsenal was set aside for chemical and weapons production, carried on here for 40 years. Production areas were surrounded by a 1-mile buffer that created an "island of habitat" for wildlife as the Denver metro area grew. The Arsenal is currently an active remediation site in transition to becoming one of the largest urban refuges in the country. Today an amazing diversity of birds, mammals, reptiles, and amphibians inhabits this pocket of undeveloped land on the edge of a major metropolitan area. Ponds and lakes, grasslands, and riparian zones are the primary areas of habitat. A bald eagle viewing blind and more than 5 miles of hiking trails are open to visitors seasonally. Guided tours and nature programs are available year-round. Three trails leave from the visitor center. The Refuge is open to visitors Saturdays and Sundays, 8 a.m. to 4:30 p.m. but access is subject to change. Contact the U.S. Fish and Wildlife Service for hours of operation and seasonal closures. **www.rockymountainarsenal.fws.gov**

Viewing information: White-tailed and mule deer are highly visible, as are coyotes, prairie dogs, Canada geese, and many species of songbirds and waterfowl. Prairie dog colonies attract a variety of raptors, including ferruginous hawks and a large population of wintering bald eagles. In summer, burrowing owls nest in the prairie dog towns. Smaller birds include Bullock's orioles, flickers, wrens, and warblers. Lakes, ponds, and surrounding marshy areas attract ducks, geese, coots, grebes, herons, avocets, and other birds. A viewing blind overlooks a bald eagle winter roost, used by the birds from early December through February.

Ownership: U.S. Army, USFWS (303-289-0930)

Size: 17,000 acres

Closest town: Denver; Commerce City; lodging, restaurants

Directions: See map next page

In winter, bald eagles and other birds of prey visit the Rocky Mountain Arsenal. The Arsenal offers snowy Front Range vistas and unparalleled wildlife viewing opportunities within 10 miles of downtown Denver.
WENDY SHATTIL/
BOB ROZINSKI

Description: An irrigation pond dating from the 1880s and later an open space buffer zone adjacent to Stapleton International Airport, Bluff Lake is now an environmental education site. Remnant short and midgrass prairie on bluffs, wetlands at the lake, and riparian habitat of cottonwoods and willows along Sand Creek. Vegetation is a mix of native grasses, wildflowers, and shrubs such as chokecherry and wild plum, and weedy exotic species. Bluff Lake Natural Area protects one of the last fragments of undisturbed shortgrass prairie in a 25-mile radius. www.blufflakenaturecenter.org

Viewing information: Wildlife is a mix of surviving prairie species, migrants, and urban wildlife. Coyotes, red foxes, mule deer, cottontails, jackrabbits, muskrats, badgers, skunks, raccoons. Reptiles include milk, garter, and bullsnakes. Watch for grassland, riparian, and marsh birds. Guided nature walks, interpretive signs, education shelter, amphitheater, boardwalk over the lake, bird blind. All trails are universally-accessible. Open daily from sunrise to sunset. **No pets or bicycles.**

Ownership: Friends of Bluff Lake (303-468-3240)

Size: 123 acres

Closest town: Denver; Aurora; in town, lodging, restaurants

Directions: See map this page

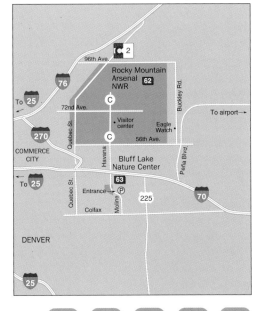

Great blue herons are a common sight along waterways as they stand motionless watching for prey. Watch as they grab prey with a lightning stab of the long bill.
CATHY AND GORDON ILLG

FRONT RANGE

81

64. RIVERSIDE CEMETERY

Description: Oldest cemetery in Denver, on National Register of Historic Places. Open, grassy lawns with scattered trees along the South Platte River, surrounded by industrial area. Cattails, some willows, scattered cottonwoods, native grasses, and weedy vegetation border ponds along the river, which runs along the west edge of the cemetery. Ponds along the river are accessible from the cemetery driveway.

Viewing information: Best viewing is along the river. Pelicans seen on the ponds in summer. Great horned owl in trees near the river. Harriers, Brewer's, and red-winged blackbirds, kestrels, abundant magpies, crows, starlings, flickers, mourning doves. Abundant waterfowl on the river including mallards, shovelers, gadwalls, green-winged teal, Canada geese. Avocets, rails, killdeer, sandpipers, and other shorebirds (in migration). Muskrats occasionally seen in the ponds. Prairie dogs burrow among the old headstones in the northeast section. Also active red fox dens. White-tailed deer sometimes come up off the river in fall. The cemetery is open 8 a.m. to 5 p.m.

Ownership: PVT (303-293-2466)

Size: 88 acres   **Closest town:** Denver, in town; lodging, restaurants

Directions: See map opposite page

65. FAIRMOUNT CEMETERY

Description: A historic cemetery in east Denver with mature nonnative urban forest. The High Line Canal, with its paved biking and walking trail, cuts through the cemetery from the south to the northeast. Water level varies. Along the bank grows a mix of cottonwoods, willows, Russian olives, and native and nonnative grasses and flowering plants. Undeveloped acreage is weedy grassland.

Viewing information: Full complement of urban bird species—crows, flickers, house finches, starlings, magpies, grackles, house sparrows, mourning doves. Winter watching includes robins, cedar waxwings, all three nuthatches, creepers, Cassin's finches, juncos, downy woodpeckers, Canada geese, great horned owls. Good place for migrant songbirds in spring and fall. Watch along the Canal for mallards, great blue herons, black-crowned night herons, Bullock's orioles, Brewer's blackbirds. Barn swallows at bridges over the canal. Active red fox dens. Glimpses of adult foxes during the day not uncommon. The kits can be seen in late spring around the dens. Best place is in open areas of the Emmanuel Cemetery within the larger cemetery. Check the small pond by the flower shop for waterfowl, red-winged blackbirds, hunting foxes.

Ownership: PVT (303-399-0692)

Size: 280 acres   **Closest town:** Denver, in town; lodging, restaurants

Directions: See map opposite page

Description: This shortgrass prairie preserve in eastern Aurora is rolling grassland with native grasses, flowering plants, and shrubs typical of the High Plains such as sagebrush, rabbitbrush, yucca, and wild rose. Some cottonwoods grow in drainages. Four replica Cheyenne tepees and four 1880s-era sod houses are used in cultural interpretive programs. Suburban development at its borders creates a juxtaposition between the prairie and encroaching city. www.plainscenter.org

Viewing information: Good place near the city to see wildlife typical of the native shortgrass prairie of eastern Colorado. Pronghorn, coyotes, prairie dogs, badgers, jackrabbits. Common reptiles include short-horned lizards, bullsnakes, western rattlesnakes. Good spot also for grassland songbirds such as meadowlarks, horned larks, and lark buntings. Red-tailed and ferruginous hawks, golden eagles common. Watch for burrowing owls in prairie dog towns. The center is open 9 a.m. to 5 p.m. Saturday. Call for times for scheduled events.

Ownership: PVT (PCC office, 303-693-3621)

Size: 2,000 acres

Closest town: Aurora, in town; lodging, restaurants

Directions: *See map this page*

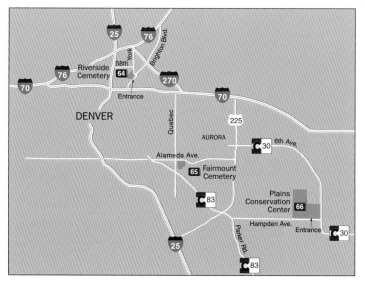

Description: Extensive remnant shortgrass prairie and old fields surround a large reservoir that receives very heavy recreational use. Riparian habitat, cattail wetlands and ponds along Cherry Creek and extensive cottonwoodland around the south end of the reservoir; grassland on drier, rolling uplands. Vegetation is a mix of remnant native plants, weedy non-native species, and agricultural remnants like alfalfa. **www.parks.state.co.us**

Viewing information: Watch in prairie areas for harriers, red-tailed hawks, pheasants, coyotes, meadowlarks. Burrowing owls in prairie dog town located in the south part of the park. Muskrats and beavers can be seen in ponds along Cherry Creek, which are very good for waterfowl in the winter, and ducks, soras, coots, red-winged and yellow-headed blackbirds in summer. In winter watch for bald eagles. Cottonwoodlands host abundant nesting songbirds. Great blue herons, black-crowned night herons are common year-round. White-faced ibis, turkey vultures, variety of swallows and songbirds are seen in migration. The open lake is very good for white pelicans, cormorants, geese, variety of ducks and gulls. Watch for nests of great horned owls and Swainson's hawks. Wetland area along Cherry Creek south of the main road is closed to dogs, horses, and bicycles. Paved walking and biking trails, nature trail, bird blind on south shore, prairie dog observation area.

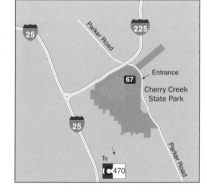

Ownership: State Parks (303-699-3860)

Size: 3,900 acres

Closest town: Aurora, in town

Directions: *See map this page*

With a large reservoir fringed by cottonwood-lands and surrounded by grasslands, Cherry Creek State Park attracts a variety of wildlife to its many habitats.
SHERM SPOELSTRA

Description: A steep-walled "prairie canyon" cut by Cherry Creek offers dramatic terrain and habitat for cliff-dwelling raptors and other birds. Rocky canyon top with ponderosa pine and scrub oak, dramatic palisades, and panoramic views up and down the canyon. Ten miles of hiking trails; maps are available. A visitor center with displays about ecology is open daily. **Do not climb on the unstable ruins of the Castlewood Dam**, which was washed out in a 1936 flood. **www.parks.state.co.us**

Viewing information: Excellent place to spot turkey vultures lazing on the thermals. Sometimes as many as 100 will congregate above the canyon. Watch also for golden eagles (nesting nearby), as well as red-tailed, Swainson's, and ferruginous hawks. Site of a unique "dry heronry" with great blue herons nesting in pine trees. Avoid approaching the nests as the herons are easily disturbed. Saw-whet owls and nesting great horned owls. Watch for dippers along the creek. Western rattlesnakes sun among the rocks. Fence lizards also common. Look for deer atop the canyon or along the creek. A variety of small mammals—cottontails, squirrels, deer mice, beavers, and muskrats—is found along the creek.

Ownership: State Parks
(303-688-5242)

Size: 1,631 acres

Closest town: Franktown, 2.5 miles; restaurants, lodging

Directions: *See map this page*

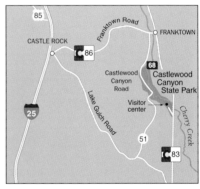

FRONT RANGE

Turkey vultures, nature's recyclers, eat animal carcasses. Their featherless heads allow easy access to their meals and prevent bacterial buildup. Dozens of these large vultures regularly soar above Castlewood Canyon.
D. ROBERT FRANZ

85

Description: The academy is a mosaic of grasslands and mixed conifers, mainly ponderosa pine, on the east. Douglas-fir on steep, north-facing slopes to the west. Riparian zone along Monument Creek. **www.usafa.af.mil**

Viewing information: Watch for elk dawn and dusk moving across the roads, particularly on North Gate Boulevard and Parade Loop. Deer are everywhere and can be a hazard on roadways. Other mammals include coyotes, foxes, and squirrels. Beavers and muskrat inhabit the creek. Great variety of birds including wild turkeys, songbirds, owls, great blue herons and waterfowl, including buffleheads. The Academy is open to visitors daily from 8 a.m. to 6 p.m. Stop at the post visitor center (open daily from 9 a.m. to 5 p.m.) for a map and directions. The Stanley Canyon and Falcon hiking trails are open 5 a.m. to sundown every day. The portion of the Santa Fe hiking trail that passes through Academy grounds is open to the public. Parking is available next to the north gate entrance.

Ownership: U.S. Air Force (visitor center, 719-333-2025)

Size: 18,500 acres   **Closest town:** Colorado Springs, in town; lodging, restaurants

Directions: *See map this page*

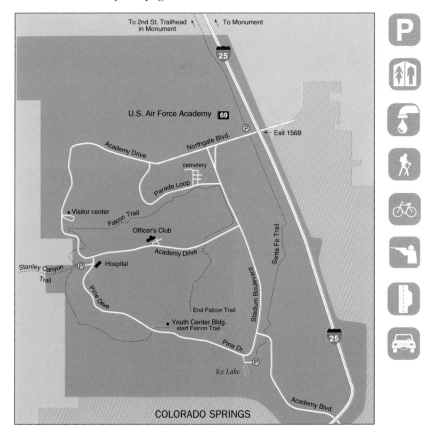

Description: Located in the foothills on the west side of Colorado Springs, the Garden of the Gods is renowned for its spectacular red sandstone formations. This foothills transition zone is the farthest north reach of piñon-juniper habitat along the Front Range, intermixed with oakbrush and grassy areas. Some riparian habitat along intermittent waterways. **www.gardenofgods.com**

Viewing information: Bighorn sheep may be seen from the main parking lot on rocky outcrops to the north. In the central garden area look high in the cliffs for nesting prairie falcons, which are year-round residents. The park is home to magpies, ravens, scrub, Steller's and blue jays, swallows, meadowlarks, spotted towhees, canyon wrens, song sparrows, solitaires, harriers, red-tailed hawks, and typical piñon-juniper birds such as juniper titmice, ash-throated flycatchers, bushtits and pinyon jays. Spectacular sunset flights of white-throated swifts in summer, visible in the central garden area. The Rockledge Ranch Historic Site across from the visitor center has a pond and wetlands with mallards and red-winged blackbirds. Over 170 species of birds have been seen in the park. Mammals include mule deer, coyotes, squirrels, cottontails, black bears, bobcats, and elk. Among reptiles that may be seen are rattlesnakes, bullsnakes, garter snakes, and fence lizards. The visitor center has a naturalist, exhibits, programs, checklists, free nature walks and a restaurant.

Ownership: City of Colorado Springs (visitor center, 719-634-6666)

Size: 1,367 acres

Closest town: Colorado Springs, in town; lodging, restaurants

Directions: *See map this page*

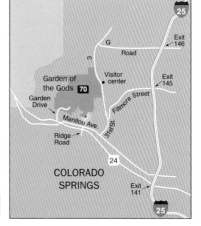

FRONT RANGE

Black bears can vary in color from black to cinnamon to blond.
TOM TIETZ

87

Description: The park combines foothills terrain dotted with Gambel oak thickets, areas of open meadows with yucca and native grasses, and cottonwood riparian zones along a creek. The nature center has interpretive displays, self-guided nature trails, interpretive programs, and naturalists on duty. www.adm.elpasoco.com/parks

Viewing information: Mule deer live in the park. Watch also for cottontails, rock squirrels, and other meadow rodents. Red foxes and coyotes may be visible. Watch for signs of raccoons, long-tailed weasels, and bear (especially in fall). Sharp-shinned, Cooper's, and goshawks in wooded areas. Spotted towhees and scrub jays abound. Watch for five races of dark-eyed junco. Warblers include yellow-rumped, McGillivray's, Virginia's, and Wilson's. Western tanagers are abundant in spring, pine siskins in winter. Nesting broad-tailed hummingbirds. Other birds include great horned owls, meadowlarks, goldfinches, Bullock's orioles, brown creepers, black-capped and mountain chickadees, and white crowned sparrows. In warm months watch for Woodhouse's toads, box turtles, hognose and garter snakes, and bullsnakes.

Ownership: El Paso County (719-520-6387)

Size: 1,235 acres

Closest town: Colorado Springs; restaurants, lodging

Directions: *See map this page*

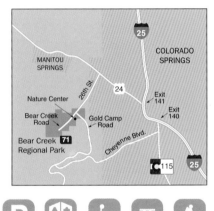

The great horned owl is known for its large size and long ear tufts. Its wing feather design enables this nocturnal hunter to fly silently through the woods.
SHERM SPOELSTRA

72. WALDO CANYON TRAIL

Description: This trail in the Pike National Forest traverses piñon-juniper woodlands intermixed with oakbrush and open meadows of native grasses and flowering plants. Mountain forests with riparian habitat in moist areas. www.fs.fed.us

Viewing information: This loop trail passes through a variety of habitats for abundant wildlife typical of foothills and lower-elevation mountain ecosystems. Watch for chipmunks, Abert's and pine squirrels, and bighorn sheep. Birds such as juncos, mountain chickadees, nuthatches, Steller's and scrub jays, flickers, sapsuckers, ravens, wild turkeys, and various sparrows, warblers, and flycatchers. Reptiles include rattlesnakes, garter snakes, and eastern fence lizards.

Ownership: USFS (719-636-1602)

Size: 7 miles, round trip

Closest town: Manitou Springs, 2 miles; lodging, restaurants

Directions: *See map this page*

73. MANITOU LAKE

Description: Mountain forest of ponderosa pine and aspen interspersed with mountain meadows located at about 8,000 feet in elevation. Manitou Lake is a five-acre reservoir with cattail wetlands. Trout Creek is lined with willow thickets. www.fs.fed.us

Viewing information: Check forested areas for mountain wildlife including Abert's squirrels, Steller's jays, pygmy nuthatches, western tanagers, and yellow-rumped warblers. Wet areas host kingfishers, beavers, a variety of waterfowl, and herons. Watch for dippers along Trout Creek. Listen for flammulated owls in the Manitou Experimental Forest. Information kiosk, campground naturalist programs, wetland boardwalk, universally-accessible fishing pier. More than half of the terrain is universally-accessible.

Ownership: USFS (719-636-1602)   **Size:** 2 miles of trail

Closest town: Woodland Park, 7 miles; lodging, restaurants

Directions: *See map this page*

Description: Higher portions of the park are high-elevation pine forest interspersed with aspen groves and mountain meadows. Spectacular vistas of Pikes Peak, Collegiate Peaks, and Sangre de Cristo Range. Rugged canyon with open southern exposures and rocky slopes above Four Mile Creek. Visitor center has interpretive displays and ranger-led hikes and programs. Eighty miles of trails, including a self-guided nature trail. www.parks.state.co.us www.wildlife.state.co.us

Viewing information: Golden eagles nest on Dome Rock. Active beaver colony along Four Mile Creek. Watch for elk in meadows. Good winter viewing of bighorn sheep along Four Mile Creek. Listen and look in the high mountain forest for birds such as dusky grouse, crossbills, Cassin's finches, pine grosbeaks, and hermit thrushes. Small mammals include chickarees, chipmunks, and weasels. The 9,000-acre **Dome Rock State Wildlife Area** near Dome Rock is a good place to look for bighorn sheep. Golden eagles have nested there for many years. Elk and deer are common.

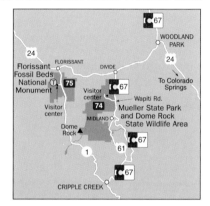

Ownership: CDOW, State Parks (719-687-2366)

Size: 12,103 acres

Closest town: Divide, 3 miles; restaurants, lodging

Directions: See map this page

Long-tailed weasels are voracious predators. Their brown coat in summer and white coat in winter help camouflage them as they prey on small mammals.
DENNIS AND MARIA HENRY

75. FLORISSANT FOSSIL BEDS NATIONAL MONUMENT TRAILS

Description: Ponderosa pine forest on drier slopes with Douglas-fir and blue spruce on cooler slopes. Grassy hillsides and meadows. The two-mile Sawmill Loop wanders through ponderosa pine and grassy valleys, with excellent views of Pikes Peak. The one-mile Hans Loop extension drops down into a wetland habitat. The four-mile Hornbek Wildlife Loop crosses meadows and wooded hillsides. **www.nps.gov**

Viewing information: The main attraction of this park is the 33- to 35-million-year-old fossil insects and plants, but the trails offer the chance to see more contemporary life forms. Despite the names, the Sawmill Loop is better than the Hornbek Wildlife Loop for wildlife sightings. Good chance for seeing elk. Watch for mule deer, pine and Abert's squirrels, Steller's jays, and other wildlife of the mountain forest. Self-guided, universally-accessible trails (challenge level 1), scheduled interpretive talks and ranger-led walks in summer, visitor center with exhibits and book sales.

Ownership: NPS (719-748-3253)

Size: 7 miles of trails

Closest town: Florissant, 2.5 miles; restaurants

Directions: See map opposite page

During the fall rut, a bull elk's antlers become important tools for challenging other males and sparring antler-to-antler.
DAVID F. TONEY

Description: This mountain driving tour along paved Park County Road 77 follows Tarryall Creek through a lush high-elevation valley of the Front Range, beginning one mile west of Lake George along the South Platte River. It traverses broad, grassy valleys flocked by rolling ponderosa pine and aspen-covered hills. The route rises to open, wet meadows of grasses and sedges around Tarryall Reservoir, dropping down to the vast, open expanse of South Park at Jefferson. **www.fs.fed.us**

Viewing information: Many large mammals may be seen on this route. Elk, mule deer, black bears, mountain lions, pronghorn (in South Park). Bighorn sheep use the meadows and mineral licks along the creek at Tarryall Reservoir. To reach the cliffs where bighorn may be seen, walk for 0.25 to 1.0 mile along forest trails from the Twin Eagle Campground trailheads. Other mammals to watch for include coyotes, cottontails, porcupines, raccoons, foxes, beavers. Excellent birding for mountain and riparian birds. Habitat stamp required to use Tarryall Creek Reservoir State Wildlife Area.

Ownership: USFS (719-836-2031), PVT   **Size:** 42 miles

Closest town: Jefferson; Lake George   *Directions: See map this page*

Description: Three reservoirs along the South Platte River in South Park—Spinney Mountain, Eleven Mile, and Antero—offer large bodies of open water habitat in this high, open mountain park. The oxbows of the river meander through rolling hills of mountain grasslands. Some wetlands around the reservoirs. South Park is ringed by high mountains with pine forests where the park rises in elevation. The reservoirs lie within Spinney Mountain State Park, Eleven Mile State Park, and Antero Reservoir State Wildlife Area, respectively. www.parks.state.co.us

Viewing information: Ducks, Canada geese, grebes, rails, and a variety of shorebirds are common, particularly during migration. White pelicans are easily seen at all three reservoirs in summer. The pelicans nest on islands in Antero Reservoir. The dam, nesting islands, and south and west shores of Antero are closed to public access. Look for mountain bluebirds, meadowlarks, horned larks in open areas. Bald and golden eagles are sometimes seen in spring and fall. Mammals that may be seen in South Park include pronghorn, elk, mule deer, coyotes, badgers, porcupines. Spinney Mountain, which is a day-use area, is closed from "ice-on" until "ice-off"—approximately November 15 to May 1. Camping is available at Eleven Mile (call Eleven Mile State Park for information and the Colorado State Parks reservation line for reservations—see General Information, page 18) and Antero. Facilities offered at the three sites vary.

Ownership: State Parks (Eleven Mile/Spinney Mountain, 719-748-3401), CDOW (303-291-7227)

Size: 17,000 acres

Closest town: Hartsel, 10 miles; Lake George, 10 miles; restaurants

Directions: *See map this page*

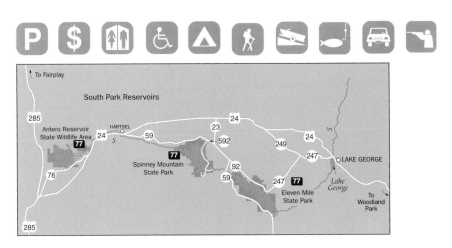

FRONT RANGE

Description: This rocky canyon on the Gold Belt Tour follows Eight Mile Creek along the former bed of the Florence and Cripple Creek Railroad, once a lifeline to the gold camps. The route starts in arid areas of native grasses and cholla cactus. Lower reaches of the canyon reveal piñon/juniper-covered slopes with cottonwoods along the water. Upper reaches of the canyon feature Engelmann spruce and subalpine fir with patches of aspen. The road is gravel, one-lane in places, and portions are confined by narrow canyon walls. Do not attempt to drive it with travel trailers, motor homes, or large campers. Interpretive exhibits at the upper and lower ends of the canyon cover wildlife, vegetation, and other topics. Geologic maps are available at the BLM office in Canon City. **www.blm.gov**

Viewing information: Watch for roadrunners in the canyon's lower end and numerous songbirds among riparian areas. Canyon species include canyon wrens, mountain bluebirds, swifts, and swallows. Watch for dusky grouse in higher-elevation forests and wild turkeys feeding near the creek early and late in the day. Cliff-nesting raptors include golden eagles, red-tailed hawks, and prairie falcons. Peregrine falcons nest in a side canyon near the Beaver Creek Wilderness Study Area. Watch for mule deer in open areas.

Ownership: PVT, BLM (719-269-8500)

Size: 15 miles, one way

Closest town: Victor, 2.5 miles; Canon City, 10 miles; restaurants, lodging

Directions: *See map opposite page*

In spite of their name, pine siskins in Colorado are more abundant in spruce/fir habitats. They are one of the ten most abundant birds in the state, nesting in loose colonies and traveling in flocks.
GEORGE H. H. HUEY

Description: Riparian habitat of cottonwoods, with a dense understory of willows and some wetlands along Beaver Creek, surrounded by old hay meadows. Uplands are mix of piñon-juniper woodlands, some ponderosa pine, and shrublands including very mature Gambel's oaks reaching 20 feet in height. Upstream, the canyon becomes very rugged and forks into two narrow canyons. Lake Skaguay reservoir lies at the north end of the west fork. The area is surrounded by BLM wilderness. Access to the upper canyon is via the town of Victor and Gold Camp Road. **www.wildlife.state.co.us**

Viewing information: Watch for a variety of mammals—mule deer, elk, ringtails (mostly nocturnal), occasional black bears. Look for bighorn sheep on hillsides and meadows, particularly in winter. This area is estimated to have the highest concentration of mountain lions in Colorado. Trout in Beaver Creek. Rock and canyon wrens in rocky habitat. Piñon jays, blue-gray gnatcatchers, spotted towhees, red-naped sapsuckers, juncos, Bewick's wrens, eastern and mountain bluebirds, loggerhead shrikes in summer, northern shrikes in winter. Raptors are common.

Ownership: CDOW (719-530-5520)

Size: 2,740 acres

Closest town: Canon City, 10 miles; restaurants, lodging

Directions: *See map this page*

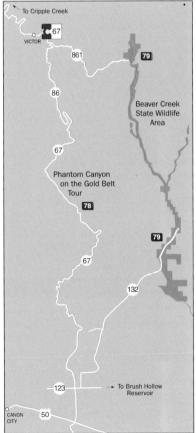

Ringtails are shy and nocturnal but may feed upon a sleeping camper's food during the night. They inhabit rocky canyon country. CLAUDE STEELMAN

Description: This Nature Conservancy preserve is a mosaic of habitat types with striking red rock outcroppings. The 4-mile loop trail passes through mixed shrublands of oakbrush and mountain-mahogany, meadows full of wildflowers and tallgrass species, and piñon-juniper habitat. Ponderosa pine in arroyos; Douglas-fir and white fir at higher elevations. Great diversity of plant life, including several species of orchids. A spur trail leads up Aiken Canyon along the intermittent Aiken Creek with large firs and ponderosas. A special plant community of piñon pine and Scribner's needlegrass has been designated globally rare. www.nature.org

Viewing information: The diversity of habitats in this foothills ecosystem attracts abundant wildlife. More than 100 species of birds have been recorded in the preserve, including western tanagers, spotted towhees, scrub jays, Virginia's warblers, various woodpeckers, orioles, wild turkeys. Good for raptors, including golden eagles. Prairie rattlesnakes are abundant. Watch also for toads. **No dogs are allowed.** The preserve is open year-round, dawn to dusk, on Saturday, Sunday, and Monday. The Field Station/Visitor Center is open Memorial Day to Labor Day on Saturday, Sunday and Monday 10 a.m.–3 p.m.; the rest of the year Sunday, 10 a.m.–3 p.m.

Ownership: TNC (719-632-0534)

Size: 1,600 acres

Closest town: Colorado Springs, 10 miles; lodging, restaurants

Directions: *See map this page*

Description: A large, diverse viewing site with ponds, grasslands, shrublands, piñon-juniper woodlands, and cottonwood riparian habitat. **A permit is required for wildlife viewing. Contact the Wildlife Office before visiting.**

Viewing information: Watch for waterbirds. Good raptor viewing includes golden eagles, prairie falcons, and hawks. Wooded areas attract a variety of songbirds. Mammals include mule deer, prairie dogs, rabbits, a unique plains elk herd and pronghorn.

Ownership: U.S. Army (719-524-5394, Wildlife Office)   **Size:** 136,000 acres

Closest town: Colorado Springs

Directions: See map above

Description: A spring/summer driving tour through an extensive piñon-juniper woodland mixed with open grassy areas and rocky habitat.

Viewing information: Excellent viewing of birds associated with piñon-juniper habitat including bushtits, juniper titmice, and blue-gray gnatcatchers. Begin the trip at the bridge at First Street, almost opposite the prison. Head south. For the first mile, look for scaled quail, ladder-backed woodpeckers, and canyon towhees. Veer right and drive past the municipal dump, stopping to bird as the road climbs into the forest. Just before topping the plateau, as the road narrows and cuts across a steep hillside, walk along the road—perhaps the best place east of the Divide for gray flycatchers and black-throated gray warblers. Continue west through Temple Canyon Park across Grape Creek (watch for riparian birds) to a road fork at the south entrance to the Royal Gorge (Road 3A), where hepatic tanagers have been seen in early summer. Follow the left fork down to Colorado Highway 50 to go back toward Canon City. Skyline Drive, a one-lane, one-way road that follows the crest of a steep hogback with great views, is on the left. Occasionally a roadrunner can be seen on the rocks. The route returns to Canon City on North 5th Street.

Ownership: City of Canon City (Parks Dept., 719-269-9028), BLM

Size: 12-mile loop

Closest town: Canon City, 1 mile; lodging, restaurants

Directions: *See map this page*

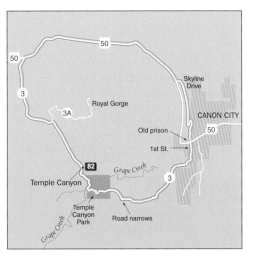

In late summer and fall, thistles provide important food for seed-eating birds such as this American goldfinch.
CATHY AND GORDON ILLG

Description: A developed interpretive facility at the Five Points Recreation Site offers information about bighorn sheep and other wildlife. Bighorn sheep are frequently visible at the recreation area. Watchable Wildlife signs throughout the canyon draw attention to other likely bighorn sheep viewing points between Parkdale and Salida. The canyon is rocky and narrow, with steep cliffs and piñon-juniper woodlands. Scenic views along the Arkansas River. Use caution and watch for other traffic when viewing the bighorn sheep. www.parks.state.co.us

Viewing information: Bighorn sheep are visible on both north- and south-facing slopes of the canyon right along the highway. Best viewing is from Coaldale to Parkdale as the bighorn sheep come down to the river to drink. Bighorn sheep can be seen year-round, but winter viewing is best. Watch also for deer and raptors, particularly bald eagles in winter.

Ownership: BLM, State Parks/Arkansas Headquarters Recreation Area (719-539-7289)

Size: 45-mile drive

Closest town: Canon City; Salida; lodging restaurants

Directions: *See map this page*

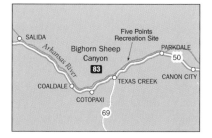

Colorado's state mammal, the Rocky Mountain bighorn sheep, is easily observed but blends well into its habitat. Look for its familiar white rump patch. The horns curl downward and the female's are spike-like. DONALD M. JONES

Description: The Pueblo Reservoir, site of both Lake Pueblo State Park (fee area) and Pueblo Reservoir State Wildlife Area, lies amid shortgrass prairie with piñon-juniper habitat on bluffs and where the terrain is more broken. Cottonwood riparian habitat below the dam along the Arkansas River. A 21-mile paved biking and walking path begins at the Greenway and Nature Center of Pueblo and follows the river, then heads up Fountain Creek. The trail connects to a 16-mile trail at Lake Pueblo State Park. The nature center has interpretive displays, an aquatic discovery center with interactive exhibits, outdoor exhibits,interpretive trails, and a naturalist on duty. The Raptor Center houses birds of prey on display Tuesday through Sunday from 11 A.M. to 4 P.M. Grounds are open sunrise to sunset. **www.gncp.org www.parks.state.co.us**

Viewing information: The nature center's fishing pier overlooks the river, offering the chance to see trout, bass, and other fish. Watch for great blue herons, kingfishers, and a variety of songbirds along the river. Ospreys are visible in spring and fall at the reservoir, and bald eagles in winter. There is one active osprey nest at the west end of the reservoir. Numerous ducks, as well as white pelicans, geese, cormorants, and grebes can be seen. Viewing of gulls, bald eagles, waterfowl, and other water birds is very good in winter. Red-tailed and Swainson's hawks are visible in open areas. Mammals include beavers, muskrats, fox squirrels, and red foxes. Excellent winter birdwatching from the Swallows Viewing Site bluffs on the north shore at the wildlife area, which has a viewing platform and interpretive signs. Directions to this site are available at the CDOW headquarters near Colorado Highway 96, south and east of the dam.

Ownership: Public/non-profit (719-549-2414)   **Size:** 21 miles, one way

Closest town: Pueblo; restaurants, lodging   *Directions: See map this page*

FRONT RANGE

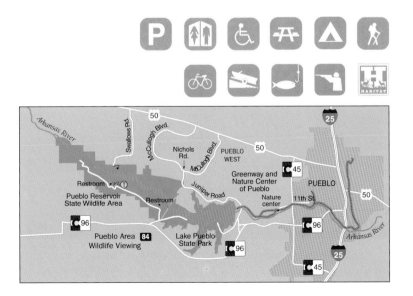

99

Description: Marshy wetlands and prairie grasslands of yucca and native grasses interspersed with piñon-juniper habitats surround two lakes—Martin and Horseshoe. Some wetlands and cottonwood/willow riparian habitats along the west side of Martin Lake. A 2-mile trail to Hogback Ridge offers good views of the area and the twin Spanish Peaks which dominate the skyline to the southwest. www.parks.state.co.us

Viewing information: The lakes and wetlands attract a variety of water birds, particularly in fall—grebes, loons, cormorants, herons, geese, dabbling and diving ducks. The bird list contains 131 species. Roadrunners are sometimes seen. The lakes contain a variety of cold- and warmwater fish, including tiger muskie, catfish, trout, bass, and bluegill. Watch for raccoons, mule deer, elk, coyotes, beavers, and muskrats. Self-guided nature trail, interpretive exhibits, bookstore, on-site naturalists, and evening programs in summer. Rattlesnakes are common.

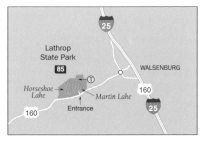

Ownership: State Parks (719-738-2376)

Size: 1,734 acres

Closest town: Walsenburg, 3 miles; lodging, restaurants

Directions: See map this page

More than 100 species of birds migrate through Lathrop State Park.
WENDY SHATTIL/ BOB ROZINSKI

Description: Named for the twin 13,000-foot peaks that rise from the High Plains of southern Colorado, the state wildlife area lies southeast of the peaks. Rugged terrain with open piñon-juniper woodlands broken by grassy meadows. Dense stands of oakbrush, ponderosa pine in moist areas, and scattered mountain-mahogany and other shrubs and forbs. Meadows good for wildflowers and butterflies. The wildlife area is divided into two parcels. The Sakariason Tract, up Sarcillo Canyon, is smaller and higher in elevation than the Oberholser/Dochter tract in adjacent Burro Canyon. www.wildlife.state.co.us

Viewing information: Wildlife plantings have encouraged wild turkeys, which are abundant in this area. Elk, mule deer, and black bears are also abundant. Small mammals include rock squirrels and jackrabbits. Songbirds include scrub, pinyon, and Steller's jays, spotted towhees, mountain and black-capped chickadees, bushtits, mountain and western bluebirds, mockingbirds, lesser goldfinches, pine siskins, various flycatchers, blue-gray gnatcatchers, black-throated gray warblers, and all three nuthatches. Watch for red-tailed and Cooper's hawks, golden eagles, turkey vultures. Sandhill cranes and white pelicans overhead during migration.

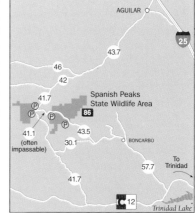

Ownership: CDOW (719-561-5300)

Size: 6,450 acres

Closest town: Aguilar, 13 miles; Trinidad, 20 miles; lodging, restaurants

Directions: *See map this page*

Often spotted in flocks or large family groups, wild turkeys roost above the ground, usually in large trees. Toms display their brilliantly colored wattles and fanned tailfeathers to attract females during the spring breeding season.
TOM TIETZ

Description: This watchable wildlife viewing area is part of Trinidad Lake State Park. A 16-acre pond with island, marshy wetlands, and cottonwood-land along a flowing tributary stream of the Purgatoire River, with grass-lands and piñon-juniper habitat on surrounding slopes, is accessed by a 0.75-mile hiking trail. No drinking water or restrooms at the viewing area. **www.parks.state.co.us**

Viewing information: Water bird and songbird viewing spring through fall. Canada geese nest on the island and grebes, various ducks, great blue herons are seen at the pond. Watch for songbirds among the cottonwoods and willows along the stream and bordering the pond, including warblers, vireos, flycatchers, goldfinches, nuthatches. In surrounding uplands look for pinyon and scrub jays, bluebirds, towhees, wild turkeys, rock wrens. Red-tailed hawks nest in the canyon. There is a large beaver lodge adjacent to the marsh. You may also see mule deer. A 0.75-mile hiking trail leads from the parking area to viewing blinds overlooking the pond and wetlands. Visitor center, bookstore, and bird list available in the main park.

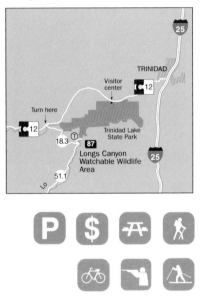

Ownership: State Parks (719-846-6951)

Size: 2,500 acres

Closest town: Trinidad, 10 miles; lodging, restaurants

Directions: *See map this page*

The marks on this aspen demonstrate the beating trees can take from the rubbing, chewing, scraping and scratching of bears, porcupines, elk, and beavers. Look for this at Bosque del Oso.
K. MAX CANESTORP

88. BOSQUE DEL OSO STATE WILDLIFE AREA

Description: Piñon-juniper woodlands with grassy meadows, oakbrush, mountain-mahogany and ponderosa pine, with Douglas-fir and white fir at higher elevations. Cottonwoods grow along the creeks and cottonwood riparian habitat and open hay meadows along the Purgatoire River. www.wildlife.state.co.us

Viewing information: Excellent site for elk as well as mule deer, mountain lions, coyotes, black bears. Very diverse bird population. Spring and summer watch for hummingbirds, a variety of woodpeckers, mockingbirds, bluebirds, and many other songbirds. Wild turkeys are abundant. Raptors include hawks, eagles, and goshawks. Variety of owls including screech, great horned, and saw-whet. Hiking access by old roads. Site is closed December 1 to April 1 to protect wintering elk, still visible from Colorado Highway 12 (see Site 89). The east side of Bosque del Oso is passable but slick in wet weather.

Ownership: CDOW (719-561-5300)

Size: 30,000 acres

Closest town: Weston, 5 miles; lodging

Directions: See map this page

FRONT RANGE

89. STONEWALL WINTERING ELK RANGE

Description: Meadows and grasslands surrounded by ponderosa pine forest. Land is private so viewing is from the county road.

Viewing information: Watch for elk in meadows and open areas along the County Road 13 between Stonewall and the New Mexico border. Wild turkeys and bald eagles can be seen along the South Fork of the Purgatoire River. Evening and early morning are best viewing times for elk and wild turkeys. Watch for birds in the meadows and among the pines.

Ownership: PVT, (CDOW for information, 719-561-5300)

Size: 16 miles, one way

Closest town: Stonewall

Directions: See map this page

103

Description: These adjacent state wildlife areas rise up the east side of Raton Mesa from the High Plains of southeastern Colorado to Fisher's Peak at 10,000 feet in elevation. Lake Dorothey is a 10-acre reservoir stocked with sport fish. Willow riparian habitats with New Mexico locust along the stream near the Lake Dorothey parking lot and downstream from the dam. Willows grow along drainages off the back side of Fisher's Peak. Moving up the mesa, habitats include piñon-juniper woodlands interspersed with grassy meadows, oakbrush, and stands of ponderosa pine, aspen and spruce/fir forest. On top is tallgrass mountain meadow. Auto access through New Mexico into a parking lot at Lake Dorothey SWA. Access to James M. John SWA by foot and horseback only. www.wildlife.state.co.us

Viewing information: Good chance of seeing migrating raptors, particularly Swainson's hawks. Peregrine falcons and golden eagles nest on the mesa's rocky cliffs. Goshawks seen regularly. Riparian areas near the lake good for warblers, wood-pewees, vireos, lesser goldfinches. Watch open areas for western and mountain bluebirds, green-tailed towhees. Only confirmed site in Colorado for acorn woodpeckers. Best chance of seeing large mammals, including mule deer, elk, mountain lions, and black bears, is on Raton Mesa. Wild turkeys in riparian areas and ponderosa pine forests. Dusky grouse at higher elevations.

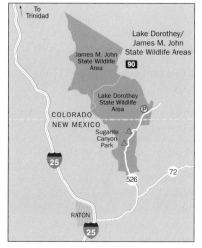

Ownership: CDOW (719-561-5300)

Size: 13,000 acres

Closest town: Raton, (New Mexico), 12 miles; lodging, restaurants

Directions: *See map this page*

Black bears are solitary animals and usually shy of humans. They are most often glimpsed in the fall, when they may spend up to 23 hours a day feeding in preparation for winter hibernation.

MACK AND SHARON JOHNSON

Rocky Mountains

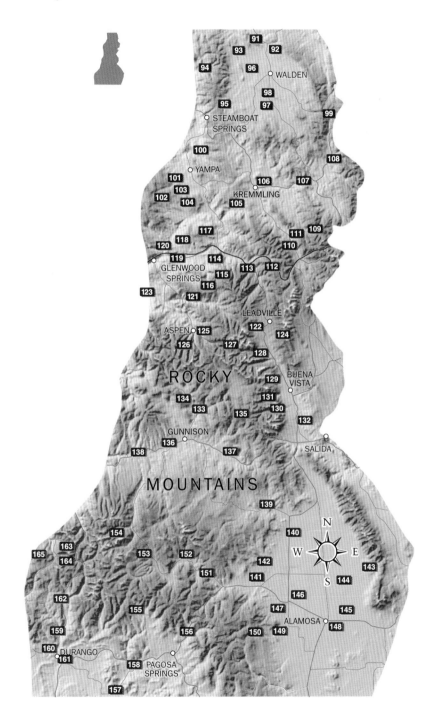

Locations: 91, 93, 92, 94, 96, WALDEN, 98, 95, 97, STEAMBOAT SPRINGS, 99, 100, YAMPA, 106, 107, 108, 101, 103, KREMMLING, 102, 104, 105, 117, 111, 109, 118, 110, 120, 119, 114, 113, 112, GLENWOOD SPRINGS, 115, 116, 123, 121, LEADVILLE, 122, ASPEN, 125, 124, 126, 127, 128, ROCKY, 129, BUENA VISTA, 131, 134, 130, 133, 135, 132, GUNNISON, 136, SALIDA, 138, 137, MOUNTAINS, 139, 140, N, 154, W, E, 163, 153, 152, 165, 164, 142, 143, S, 151, 141, 144, 162, 146, 155, 147, 145, 159, 156, 150, 149, ALAMOSA, 148, 160, DURANGO, 161, 158, PAGOSA SPRINGS, 157

The Rocky Mountains contain a diverse mix of forests, mountain meadows, wetlands, open parks, and rocky cliffs. Forests of ponderosa pine and Douglas-fir blend into Engelmann spruce and subalpine fir at higher

elevations, intermixed with bright stands of aspen and dark lodgepole pine forests. At the very top of Colorado lies the austere, slow-growing world of the alpine tundra.

91. NORTHGATE CANYON NATURE TRAIL

Description: A nature trail beginning in a dry shrubland of bitterbrush, big sagebrush, and serviceberry with limber pine, piñon, and juniper on hot, south-facing slopes and Douglas-fir, ponderosa, and lodgepole pine on cooler, moister slopes. The trail descends into the canyon of the North Platte River. Riparian habitat along the river. **www.fs.fed.us**

Viewing information: Badgers, elk, mule deer, white-tailed prairie dogs, jackrabbits, coyotes, pronghorns inhabit uplands. The shrubs offer good winter forage for grazing mammals. You may see pine squirrels, porcupines, and snowshoe hares in woodlands. Check the riparian habitat for beavers, muskrats, herons and other shorebirds, warblers and songbirds. Waterfowl can be seen on the river. Check riverside rocks for spotted sandpipers. Other birds include blue and sage grouse, magpies, ravens, turkey vultures, mountain bluebirds, kestrels, mountain chickadees, and flickers.

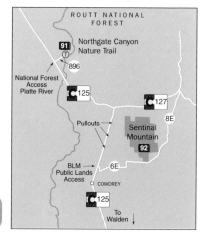

Ownership: USFS (970-723-8204)

Size: 1-mile trail

Closest town: Cowdrey, 8 miles

Directions: *See map this page*

92. SENTINAL MOUNTAIN

Description: Sagebrush grasslands with stands of aspen and a few conifers at the top of the mountain, which rises from 8,000 to 9,082 feet. The north and east sides of Sentinal Mountain burned in the late 1980s, and the resultant growth created excellent elk habitat.

Viewing information: Good elk viewing from pullouts along Colorado Highway 125. Mid-November to mid-April scan the mountainsides for elk. About 400 animals use this area for winter range. If snow cover is heavy, the animals feed more on east- and south-facing slopes. A spotting scope or good binoculars often necessary. Watch also for pronghorn, golden eagles, prairie and possibly peregrine falcons, red-tailed and Swainson's hawks.

Ownership: North Park Chamber of Commerce (970-723-4600), CDOW Walden Work Center (970-723-4625), BLM

Size: 1,400 acres

Closest town: Cowdrey, 3 miles

Directions: *See map this page*

Description: High mountain lakes surrounded by forests of lodgepole pine and spruce/fir coming down to the water's edge. Good hiking trails lead through a glacial moraine with several kettle lakes. Open mountain meadows with alder/willow riparian zones. Outstanding scenic area with extensive recreational opportunities. Along the rolling hills before Big Creek Lake there are impressive limber pine woodlands along the ridges, with unusual flora and showy wildflower displays in early summer. Various orchids bloom in the spruce/fir forests around the upper Big Creek Lakes, including clustered lady's slipper. Also trillium and a good variety of pyrolas and wintergreens. www.fs.fed.us

Viewing information: Excellent opportunity to view ospreys hovering over the lakes and plunging into the water feet first to catch fish. Nesting begins in May and young are flying by August. Loons have been sighted on the lake in the fall. Watch for ducks on the kettle lakes, including buffleheads. Other water-associated birds include black-crowned night-herons, great blue herons, killdeer, kingfishers, and spotted sandpipers. Sharp-shinned, Swainson's, and red-tailed hawks are common raptors. Lots of songbirds in the woods and riparian areas near water. Mammals include marmots, pikas, and chickarees; lots of beaver activity in the area. Watch for moose among the willows, as well as deer and elk. Fee for parking.

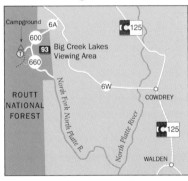

Ownership: USFS (970-723-8204)

Size: 600 acres

Closest town: Walden; restaurants, lodging

Directions: See map this page

Fish-eating ospreys typically nest in trees. However, the ospreys found in the Big Creek Lakes area nest on a manmade platform constructed in a tree.
MARK A. AUTH/
N.E. STOCK

ROCKY MOUNTAINS

Description: Located in a lush, green mountain valley, the park surrounds a lake built on four mountain streamcourses—Mill, Larsen, Floyd, and Dutch creeks. Mountain meadows and forests dominated by lodgepole pine intermixed with aspen stands with shrublands of big sagebrush, rabbitbrush, bitterbrush, currant, juniper, grass, and wildflowers. Wetlands and riparian habitats established around the reservoir and along tributaries. www.parks.state.co.us

Viewing information: Sandhill cranes nest along riparian areas; **be sure not to disturb adult cranes, nests, or young**. More than 200 species of birds recorded in the area including ravens, gray jays, dusky grouse, mountain blue-birds, goshawks, ospreys, and a variety of waterfowl and shorebirds. Look for the great blue heron nesting colony along the lakeshore. Mule deer and elk are common, as well as snowshoe hares, chickarees, porcupines, beavers, red foxes, coyotes, and muskrats. Rainbow, brook, and cutthroat trout inhabit the lake. Visitor center with interpretive exhibits, bookstore, summer programs. The 0.75-mile Tombstone Nature Trail has self-guided brochure. Nearby **Pearl Lake State Park**, east of Road 129, is a good place to see mule deer and elk, snowshoe hares, chickarees, porcupines, beavers, and coyotes, as well as ravens, blue grouse, and osprey.

Ownership: State Parks (970-879-3922)

Size: 2,553 acres

Closest town: Clark, 8 miles; lodging, restaurants

Directions: See map this page

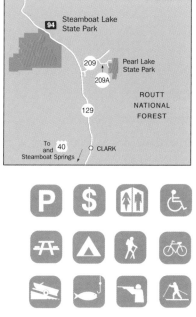

Sandhill cranes nest in wet meadows in northwestern Colorado. They feed on insects, frogs, snakes, grain, crayfish, wetland-nesting songbirds, and a variety of other food. LEE KLINE

Description: Mountain riparian area of kettle lakes and beaver ponds. Lodgepole pine and spruce/fir forests completely surround the lakes, with willow bottoms around the beaver ponds. Electric motor or hand-propelled boats only. www.fs.fed.us

Viewing information: Watch for buffleheads, mallards, ring-necked ducks, and green-winged teal. Many broad-tailed hummingbirds inhabit the campground as well as chipmunks, golden-mantled ground squirrels, and goshawks. Songbirds include yellow-rumped warblers, white-crowned sparrows, western wood pewees, Cassin's finches, and ruby-crowned kinglets. Raptors include red-tailed hawks and harriers. Elk, deer, and porcupines may be seen in the evening from the road.

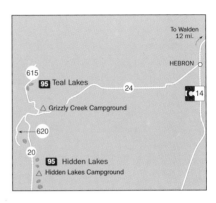

Ownership: USFS (970-723-8204)

Size: 1,000 acres

Closest town: Walden, 29 miles; restaurants, lodging

Directions: See map this page

The reintroduction of moose into northern Colorado is a great wildlife success story. Moose have since also been released in the San Juan Mountains of southern Colorado. CLAUDE STEELMAN

ROCKY MOUNTAINS

96. SHEEP MOUNTAIN RAPTORS

Description: A series of steep, rocky cliffs and outcrops along the west face of a hogback-like formation, with some cliff faces 200 feet high. Sagebrush grasslands and irrigated hay meadows at the base of the mountain. **www.fs.fed.us**

Viewing information: Excellent spring and summer viewing of raptors that nest along the cliffs and are readily viewed soaring and gliding along the mountain. Watch for golden eagles, prairie falcons, and red-tailed hawks. The mountain is mostly on private land so view from County Road 12 near the base of the mountain. **Do not approach or climb the cliffs or otherwise disturb the nesting birds.** Binoculars and spotting scopes will give good viewing of the birds and their habitats.

Ownership: BLM (970-724-3437), PVT

Size: about 4 miles of road viewing

Closest town: Walden, 12 miles; lodging, restaurants

Directions: See map this page

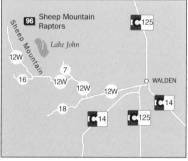

97. HEBRON WATERFOWL MANAGEMENT AREA

Description: Numerous small ponds and manmade lakes dot this 4,700-acre area, varying from less than one acre to the very large Eighteen Islands Reservoir of more than 160 surface acres. The lakes are rimmed by wetland vegetation. Surrounding uplands are grasslands dominated by sagebrush and greasewood. **www.blm.gov**

Viewing information: The small and large bodies of water within North Park attract a variety of waterfowl, particularly during spring migration. Many nest within the management area. Over 100 species of birds have been recorded here, including a variety of songbirds. Common water birds include mallards, pintails, gadwalls, wigeons, Canada geese, willets, black-crowned night herons, phalaropes, avocets, and stilts. Good site for raptors such as golden eagles, prairie falcons, harriers, and Swainson's hawks. Pronghorn can be seen year-round, mule deer and elk mainly in winter. **Vehicle access restricted to County Road 34 during June and July to protect nesting birds.**

Ownership: BLM (970-724-3437)   **Size:** 4,700 acres

Closest town: Walden, 16 miles; lodging, restaurants

Directions: See map opposite page

Description: Open ponds and irrigated meadows offer excellent habitat for nesting waterfowl, shorebirds, and marsh birds. Upland areas of sagebrush flats and knolls. Areas of trees and shrubs along the Illinois River provide excellent birdwatching and chances to see moose. **www.arapaho.fws.gov**

Viewing information: Spring and summer offer outstanding viewing of waterfowl and shore and marsh birds. Peak waterfowl migration in late May. Sage grouse, pronghorn, prairie dogs, and mule deer utilize upland sagebrush areas. Summer raptors include Swainson's hawks, northern harriers, and kestrels. Golden eagles are resident. Muskrats, Wyoming ground squirrels, jackrabbits, and coyotes are all common. Moose and elk are found along the Illinois River. A six-mile self-guided auto tour with accompanying brochure provides an excellent introduction to both upland and wetland habitats and species. A 0.5 mile interpretive nature trail along the Illinois River near the Refuge headquarters offers the chance to see moose, beavers, and otters. Nearby **Walden Reservoir** is very good for shorebirds in spring and fall. Avocets are commonly seen feeding in shallow water. Good habitat for Canada geese, dabbling and diving ducks.

Ownership: USFWS (970-723-8202), BLM

Size: 23,244 acres

Closest town: Walden, 1.5 miles; restaurants, lodging

Directions: See map this page

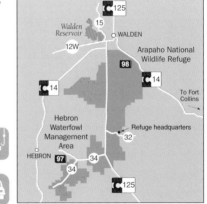

The Illinois River meanders through the Arapaho National Wildlife Refuge in northwest Colorado. Moose can be viewed in the refuge and surrounding area.
JACK OLSON

Description: Ranging in elevation from 8,500 to 12,500 feet, the state forest offers diverse forest, meadow, brush, and riparian habitats. Alpine tundra habitat above 11,000 feet. The Medicine Bow Mountains border the State Forest to the east and the Never Summer Mountains to the south. www.parks.state.co.us

Viewing information: A great variety of mountain wildlife species including moose, elk, mule deer, bighorn sheep, black bears, golden eagles, dusky grouse, and northern goshawks. Ducks, grebes, geese, terns, and gulls attracted to lakes and waterways. Great variety of songbirds. River otters sometimes seen along the Michigan River. In winter watch at lower elevations for moose, elk, deer, and white-tailed ptarmigan. Largest concentration of moose in the state. The Moose Center along Colorado Highway 14 one mile east of Gould has interpretive displays and checklists. Two self-guided nature trails, self-guided auto tour. Viewing deck seven miles into the State Forest along County Road 41 overlooks a marshy area. Nature walks, on-site naturalists, and campfire programs in summer.

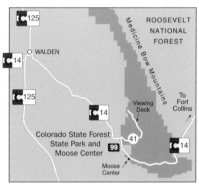

Ownership: State Parks (970-723-8366), Colorado State Board of Land Commissioners

Size: 70,768 acres in the state forest

Closest town: Walden, 23 miles; lodging, restaurants

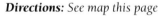

Directions: See map this page

The dusky grouse, formerly known as the blue grouse, inhabits coniferous forests of the foothills and mountains from the Front Range west across the state. Often considered "tame," dusky grouse freeze instead of flushing and can sometimes be easily viewed for long periods.
LEE KLINE

100. STAGECOACH STATE PARK WETLAND HABITAT PRESERVE

Description: A 3-mile-long reservoir along the Yampa River surrounded by rolling mountain grasslands, sagebrush shrublands, and surrounding forested mountainsides of lodgepole pine and aspen. A constructed wetland preserve of seven ponds and ditches above the reservoir is characterized by grasses, sedges, rushes, willow, and alder. www.parks.state.co.us

Viewing information: Two viewing blinds on platforms overlooking two of the ponds. Boardwalk passing through the wetlands and along the river leads to two wheelchair-accessible fishing piers. Fish in the reservoir include rainbow, brown, brook, and Snake River cutthroat trout, kokanee salmon, and northern pike. Good birding spring through fall, particularly for water birds—snipes, soras, Virginia rails, great blue herons in wetlands; mallards, geese, wigeons, green-winged and cinnamon teal on the water. Sandhill cranes feed in wet meadows and there has been one active sandhill nest at the site. **Be sure not to approach nests or young birds.** Red-tailed hawks are common and ospreys and bald and golden eagles are seen occasionally.

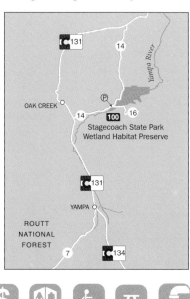

Ownership: State Parks (970-736-2436)

Size: 77 acres

Closest town: Oak Creek, 4 miles; lodging, restaurants

Directions: *See map this page*

Through spring and summer, watch for common snipe "winnowing" over wet meadows. Flying wide circles, the birds produce an eerie whirring as air rushes through their fanned tail feathers.
WENDY SHATTIL/ BOB ROZINSKI

Description: This 82-mile scenic drive between Yampa and Meeker travels from river bottomlands to high mountain forests across the Flat Tops plateau, an area pockmarked with natural lakes. It traverses a variety of habitats—stream riparian, sagebrush grasslands, mountain shrublands of serviceberry, chokecherry, and oakbrush, lodgepole pine, aspen, and subalpine fir-Engelmann spruce forest. Much of the Flat Tops is characterized by silver-gray standing dead trees resulting from a spruce bark beetle infestation in the 1940s and 1950s. Approximately 40 miles of the byway is unpaved but accessible in summer by passenger car. The byway receives two to ten feet of snow in winter and is not maintained for automobiles but is open to snowmobiles and cross-country skiing. **www.coloradobyways.org**

Viewing information: Bald eagles commonly seen along the White River in winter. Flat Tops plateau inhabited by one of the largest elk herds in Colorado. Cavity-nesting birds abundant due to standing dead trees. Warblers, fly-catchers, bluebirds, and other songbirds in riparian areas. Watch for coyotes, jackrabbits, mule deer, sage grouse, ground squirrels, rattlesnakes, red-tailed hawks, golden eagles. **Beware of herds of cattle and sheep being moved along the byway** between summer and winter pasture. Without stops, plan on a 2.5-hour drive. Gas available in Yampa, Buford, and Meeker only. Maps and information available at the Blanco Ranger District Office in Meeker and the Yampa Ranger District office in Yampa.

Ownership: USFS (Blanco Ranger District, 970-878-4039; Yampa Ranger District, 970-638-4516), State of Colorado, PVT

Size: 82 miles

Closest town: Meeker, Yampa; lodging, restaurants

Directions: *See map this page*

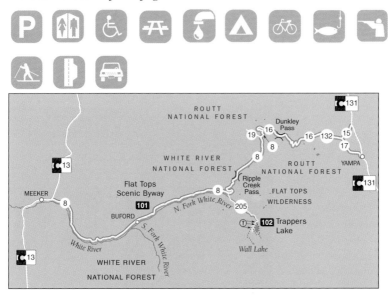

Description: A 300-acre natural lake located in the Flat Tops Wilderness at 9,627 feet in elevation. The surrounding subalpine fir-Engelmann spruce forest suffered an extensive kill in the 1940s and 1950s from spruce bark beetle disease. Known as the silver forest, it has abundant silver-gray standing dead trees that offer habitat for cavity nesting birds. Wall Lake lies 3.5 miles away along a steep switchback trail up the rim wall of the Flat Tops Plateau through high-elevation meadows. **www.fs.fed.us**

Viewing information: A variety of water birds including mallards, common mergansers, cinnamon teal, scaup. Watch for woodland birds including three-toed and downy woodpeckers, olive-sided flycatchers, golden-crowned kinglets and boreal owls (more likely heard than seen). One of the highest elevation nesting populations of Barrow's goldeneyes. Trappers Lake is home to a nearly pure strain of native Colorado River cutthroat trout. At **Wall Lake** in mid-summer, broods of goldeneyes, lesser scaup, and ring-necked ducks are common. **Hikers should beware of the risk of falling trees, particularly in windy weather.** Wall Lake trail is outstanding for wildflowers in July and August. Summer "fireside chats" by USFS naturalists. Information and maps available at Blanco Ranger District office in Meeker.

Ownership: USFS (970-878-4039)

Size: 5,000 acres

Closest town: Meeker, 50 miles; lodging, restaurants

Directions: See map opposite page

ROCKY MOUNTAINS

The elk herd inhabiting the White River region is the largest in the state of Colorado. DANIEL LARSON

117

103. GARDNER PARK INTERPRETIVE TRAIL

Description: This short, self-guided nature walk, passes along the shores of Gardner Park Reservoir. Open water habitat with marshy wetlands. Mountain forests, mountain meadows, alpine habitat on high peaks surround the site. Numerous trailheads access the Flat Tops Wilderness. **www.fs.fed.us**

Viewing information: The reservoir attracts a variety of waterfowl in summer and fall including mallard, wigeon, goldeneye, ring-necked, and ruddy ducks. Shorebirds, particularly in migration, include killdeer, snipe, and various sandpipers. Beaver and muskrats inhabit the reservoir. Watch for elk and mule deer, especially at dawn and dusk. Area closed May 15 to June 15 during elk calving season. Road access limited until mid-June.

Ownership: USFS (970-638-4516)

Size: 100 yards

Closest town: Yampa, 17 miles; lodging, restaurants

Directions: See map this page

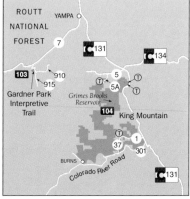

104. KING MOUNTAIN

Description: Shrublands intermixed with grasslands and piñon-juniper woodlands at lower elevations, rising into lodgepole pine and aspen forests and grassy mountain meadows. Marshy wetlands and wooded riparian habitat along streams and at several reservoirs. In addition to hiking trails, numerous four-wheel-drive side roads allow access to the area. **www.blm.gov**

Viewing information: Sage grouse inhabit shrublands dominated by big sagebrush. Higher up dusky grouse are found in aspen and lodgepole pine forests. Check the reservoirs for waterfowl. Also phalaropes, sandpipers, and other shorebirds during migration. Breeding songbirds include yellow-rumped and Wilson's warblers, green-tailed towhees, a variety of sparrows, lark buntings, pine grosbeaks, red crossbills. Woodpeckers common in woodlands. Good for raptor viewing. Mule deer, elk, black bear, cottontails, ground squirrels. Chorus and leopard frogs, tiger salamanders in moist areas.

Ownership: BLM (970-947-2800)   **Size:** 12,000 acres

Closest town: Yampa, 15 miles; lodging, restaurants

Directions: See map above

105. TROUGH ROAD

Description: Twenty-eight mile drive along Trough Road (County Road 1) from Kremmling to State Bridge along the Colorado River. The route climbs open sagebrush hillsides before descending through mixed conifer woodlands, with aspen on higher parts and cottonwood groves on the valley floor. Dirt road is suitable for passenger cars in dry weather. **www.blm.gov**

Viewing information: Prime wintertime viewing of mule deer and elk. The route passes **Radium State Wildlife Area**, considered some of the finest deer and elk winter range in the state. Watch for bald eagles along the river December to April. Other raptors may be seen in open areas, with jays and mountain chickadees in wooded areas. Red-tailed hawks, golden eagles, turkey vultures, mountain bluebirds, red-naped sapsuckers, and tree and violet-green swallows are summer residents. Waterfowl along the Colorado River include Canada geese, mallards, mergansers. Camping and restrooms are off the main road and open in summer only. Fees for camping and day use. Habitat stamp required to use the State Wildlife Area.

Ownership: BLM (970-724-3437), CDOW, PVT

Size: 28-mile drive

Closest town: Kremmling; restaurants, lodging

Directions: See map this page

106. KREMMLING PRONGHORN VIEWING SITE

Description: Excellent pronghorn viewing in rolling, open sagebrush habitat. **Stay on the county road while viewing because the animals in places are on private land.** www.blm.gov

Viewing information: Pronghorn inhabit the area year-round. Large groups begin to assemble in late summer. The animals gather in huge numbers in fall and winter. Watch for animals on the east side of County Road 22 just north of Kremmling.

Ownership: BLM (970-724-3437)

Size: 4-mile drive

Closest town: Kremmling, 3 miles; restaurants, lodging

Directions: See map above

Description: This developed wildlife viewing area overlooks a small, scenic mountain reservoir surrounded by riparian habitat. Uplands are sagebrush-dominated grassland. **www.blm.gov**

Viewing information: The viewing site is open May 1 through September 30, offering visitors prime viewing of migrating waterfowl and water birds, including western grebes, Canada geese, mallards, ring-necked ducks, lesser scaup, canvasbacks, white pelicans, cormorants. Good chance to see osprey that nest to the north and often feed in the area. Golden and bald eagles can be seen soaring over and around the reservoir. Watch also for turkey vultures and red-tailed hawks. Gulls, shorebirds, and songbirds can be seen. Mammals in the area include pronghorn, mule deer, occasional elk and moose, cottontails, jackrabbits, beavers, ground squirrels, coyotes, badgers, possible river otters, and small mammals. Watch for tiger salamanders, chorus and leopard frogs and garter snakes. Information kiosks, interpretive panels along a universally-accessible trail.

Ownership: CDOW (970-725-6200), Municipal Subdistrict of the Northern Colorado Water Conservancy District, BLM

Size: 5 acres

Closest town: Granby, 2 miles; lodging, restaurants

Directions: See map this page

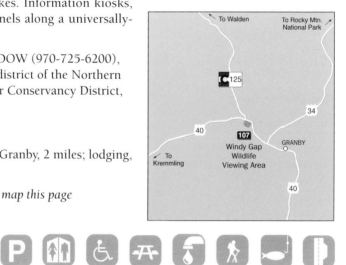

In spring watch for the elegant courtship dance of western grebes. A pair swims side by side like mirror images, bowing, looking away and back, then rising up together and running across the water.
CATHY AND GORDON ILLG

Description: This picnic site along the shore of Shadow Mountain Lake is surrounded by lodgepole pine forest coming down to the water's edge, with willow/cattail/sedge wetlands along the water's edge. Several offshore islands are accessible by canoe. **Observe the seasonal closure signs and avoid those islands where osprey are nesting.** Interpretive signs address habitat diversity, moose, osprey. Contact the USFS district office at Granby for further information and dates of seasonal closures. **www.fs.fed.us**

Viewing information: Watch for ospreys hunting on the reservoir from May to September. You may observe their nests on offshore islands with binoculars. Bald eagles are often seen in winter. Excellent beaver viewing at dusk (summer); watch for them swimming in the channels. A beaver lodge directly east of the wetlands is visible with binoculars. Otters may be seen at dusk. Excellent waterfowl viewing. Migrants include goldeneyes, scaups, buffleheads, ruddy ducks, green and blue-winged teal, pintails, and other dabbling ducks, grebes, and loons. A viewing platform at the **Double A Bar Ranch** offers good views of osprey in spring and summer and eagles in summer and winter. River otters are sometimes spotted in winter. Also waterfowl, elk, deer, moose, foxes, coyotes year-round. Songbirds in spring and summer, black bears in fall. The viewing platform is open all year but **the river and adjacent habitat immediately downstream are closed to all human use November 15 through March 1 to protect the eagles.**

Ownership: USFS (970-887-4100)

Size: 10 acres

Closest town: Grand Lake, 3 miles; restaurants, lodging

Directions: *See map this page*

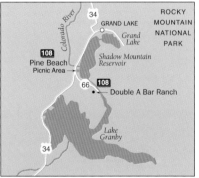

ROCKY MOUNTAINS

Scattered crayfish skeletons and fishy odors indicate the presence of the river otter. This endangered Colorado species has been reintroduced to major rivers around the state.
ART WOLFE

121

Description: The 2,500-foot-long boardwalk crosses the Williams Fork River through a series of beaver ponds and marshy wetlands, and passes through a combination of lodgepole pine forest, aspen stands, and alder/willow bottoms. Lateral boardwalks, three viewing decks built over the stream, and several seating areas facilitate viewing at the beaver ponds. The entire boardwalk and the trail to the campground are universally-accessible. **www.fs.fed.us**

Viewing information: Great access to mountain riparian area. Lots of beaver activity. Beaver viewing at dawn and dusk—dams, lodges, and other signs are very visible. Boardwalk over pools allows good views of brook and rainbow trout. Watch for squirrels, rabbits, chipmunks, and other small mammals in the campground. Deer and elk occasionally visible. Hummingbirds, warblers, and other songbirds are seen among the willows, and dippers and spotted sandpipers along the river.

Ownership: USFS (970-887-4100)

Size: 360 acres

Closest town: Parshall, 19 miles

Directions: *See map this page*

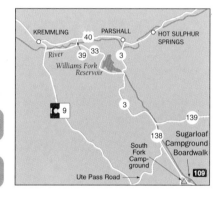

Brook trout, not native to Colorado, are popular with sportsmen. "Brookies" favor smaller coldwater streams. KEN ARCHER

110. ALFRED M. BAILEY BIRD NESTING AREA

Description: Willow-dominated wet meadow in a valley surrounded by slopes of spruce/fir and aspen. The trail from the parking lot passes through lodge-pole pine forest. The site is located in the Eagles Nest Wilderness Area and is an active study area. Please observe all wilderness rules and respect any research being done. **www.fs.fed.us**

Viewing information: The convergence of a multitude of habitats makes this a prime site for bird watching. Forty-three breeding species have been documented. Watch for pine siskins, red-naped and Williamson's sapsuckers, broad-tailed and rufous hummingbirds, Wilson's, McGillivray's, and yellow-rumped warblers, and a variety of flycatchers, finches, sparrows, and other songbirds. To view bird banding, and possibly help out, contact the Rocky Mountain Bird Observatory, (303-659-4348)

Ownership: USFS (970-468-5400)

Size: 640 acres

Closest town: Silverthorne, 11 miles; restaurants, lodging

Directions: See map this page

111. BLUE RIVER STATE WILDLIFE AREA

Description: Three parcels of mountain riparian habitat along the Blue River and its tributary creeks, surrounded by sagebrush uplands, irrigated hay meadows, and forested slopes of aspen and mixed conifers. **www.wildlife.state.co.us**

Viewing information: Numerous songbirds along the river. Watch for dippers and goldeneyes along the water in winter, warblers among the willows in summer and dusky grouse in wooded areas year-round. Great blue herons and sandpipers are occasionally sighted. Other waterfowl include mallards, teal, mergansers, and Canada geese. Golden eagles are sometimes seen in summer, bald eagles in winter. Other raptors include ospreys, kestrels, red-tailed hawks, and an occasional prairie falcon. Weasels, raccoons, foxes, river otters, and beavers use the area. Watch for deer and elk in lowlands in winter. There is a 0.5-mile nature trail with interpretive signs at the south edge of Green Mountain Reservoir. One of the parcels is universally-accessible.

Ownership: CDOW (970-725-6200)

Size: 111 acres

Closest town: Silverthorne, 10 miles; restaurants, lodging

Directions: See map above

123

Description: Rocky, grassy mountain slopes north of Interstate 70 with aspen and mixed conifer forests and mountain shrublands of sagebrush, grasses, and flowering plants. These south-facing slopes are the last remaining big game winter range in the Vail Valley and have been identified as critical to elk, mule deer, and bighorn sheep. A fall-winter viewing site.

Viewing information: In winter, from the Ford Park parking lot, scan rocky outcrops across the interstate for bighorn sheep. Watch the aspen forests and open shrublands for elk and mule deer. In above-average snow years, bighorn may move onto winter range early offering the chance to witness the breeding rut when rams battle each other. The sound of their horns clashing can be heard over the traffic noise of the highway. **Visitors must be sure not to approach the sheep or enter this critical winter habitat.**

Ownership: CDOT, Town of Vail
(USFS 970-827-5715)

Size: 4,000 acres

Closest town: Vail, in town; lodging, restaurants

Directions: *See map this page*

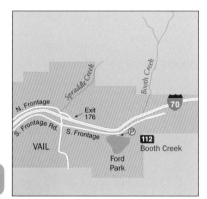

November and December are the times to witness the battle of bighorn sheep rams as the males compete for ewes during the mating season. The clash of their horns as they butt heads can be heard a mile or more away. TOM TIETZ

Description: Steep, southwest-facing slopes covered with mountain shrubs—mountain mahogany, chokecherry, and serviceberry—and small stands of aspen and lodgepole pine. The Eagle River runs along the base. **www.fs.fed.us**

Viewing information: Winter range for several hundred elk. Good viewing from U.S. Highway 24. The animals are found in draws during the day, moving to open slopes to feed in morning and evening. Visit the viewing area with telescope and platform at the Holy Cross Ranger District office.

Ownership: USFS (970-827-5715)

Size: 1,000 acres

Closest town: Minturn, 3 miles

Directions: *See map this page*

This bull is "bugling"—a high-pitched sound which is part of the glamorous species' fall mating ritual. Colorado has the largest population of elk in the United States.
DENNIS HENRY

ROCKY MOUNTAINS

125

Description: This viewing site, situated on the side of a small mountain with a mix of grassland and aspen forests, overlooks 30,000 acres of the West Divide Creek watershed in the White River National Forest. Views of mixed habitats of spruce-fir forest, aspen, mountain meadows, and shrublands, with outstanding fall colors. **www.fs.fed.us**

Viewing information: Numerous raptors can be seen, particularly during fall migration—mid-September through October. Red-tailed, Swainson's, and Cooper's hawks, northern goshawks, golden eagles, kestrels, merlins. Variety of songbirds such as white-crowned sparrows, vesper sparrows, tree and violet-green swallows, yellow-rumped warblers, and spotted towhees. Watch for elk, mule deer, and black bears. Information, maps, and checklist available at the Rifle Ranger District office in Rifle. **The road to the site is inaccessible during winter and spring and when road is wet.**

Ownership: USFS (970-625-2371)

Size: 1 acre

Closest town: Silt, 15 miles; lodging, restaurants

Directions: *See map this page*

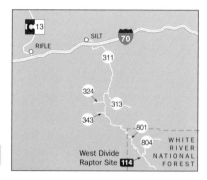

Golden eagles prey on rodents and jackrabbits and may be injured by motorists as they gather on roads to feed on roadkill. They can have a wingspan of seven feet. W. PERRY CONWAY

Description: Glacial valley surrounded by slopes of high-elevation forest, with sagebrush on lower slopes. Extensive wet meadows along East Brush Creek. Thick spruce/fir forests cover the north-facing slopes, with aspen on the south-facing slopes. Extensive recreational opportunities include camping, fishing, hunting, mountain biking, and cross-country skiing. **www.fs.fed.us**

Viewing information: An extensive beaver colony at the upper end of the valley offers good evening viewing, sometimes with two to three colonies active. Best viewed from the south side just below Fulford Cave Road (Forest Road 418). Good opportunity to see brook and rainbow trout in very clear pools. Elk wintering range. Watch for small mammals such as chickarees, marmots, and rock and golden-mantled ground squirrels. You may see signs of coyotes, weasels, and bears. Northern harriers and Swainson's and red-tailed hawks common. Keep an eye out for woodland hawks like Cooper's, sharp-shinned, and goshawks. Some waterbirds can be seen—mainly sandpipers in wet meadows, mallards, and an occasional merganser.

Ownership: USFS (970-328-6388)

Size: 1,000 acres

Closest town: Eagle, 10 miles; restaurants, lodging

Directions: *See map this page*

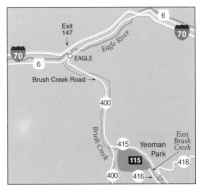

Nature's engineer, the beaver, plays a habitat construction role important to other species. Beaver dams form ponds that become home to fish, mammals, and birds.
DENNIS HENRY

ROCKY MOUNTAINS

116. SYLVAN LAKE STATE PARK

Description: Located within a bowl along West Brush Creek, the lake and encircling park lie at 8,500 feet surrounded by diverse mountain habitats. Douglas-fir, lodgepole pine, and aspen forests broken by mountain meadows of grasses and wildflowers, shrublands, mountain riparian woodlands and wetlands. **www.parks.state.co.us**

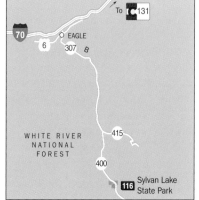

Viewing information: Watch for mule deer and the occasional black bear in summer and fall. Best time for elk is late fall and early winter, particularly on the east side of the park. Raccoons, chipmunks, ground squirrels, pocket gophers, porcupines, cottontails, beavers, muskrats, coyotes also common in summer and fall. Watch for golden eagles, red-tailed hawks, turkey vultures.

Ownership: State Parks (970-328-2021)   **Size:** 155 acres

Closest town: Eagle, 16 miles; lodging, restaurants

Directions: See map this page

117. COLORADO RIVER ROAD

Description: This self-guided auto tour along the Colorado River between Dotsero and Burns passes through rugged cliffs and rock formations and a variety of habitats. Shrublands, piñon-juniper woodlands, semi-desert shrublands. Cottonwood/willow community along the river's edge. **www.fs.fed.us**

Viewing information: In winter and spring, watch for golden eagles hunting along the cliffs and bald eagles along the river. Canada geese and waterfowl throughout the year. Mule deer and elk winter through summer. Look for mud nests of cliff swallow colonies along the cliffs above the river. The river attracts osprey, sandhill cranes, and egrets in summer. Bighorn sheep on grassy slopes in winter.

Ownership: USFS (970-947-2800), BLM   **Size:** 20,000 acres

Closest town: Glenwood Springs, 18 miles; Eagle, 13 miles; lodging, restaurants

Directions: See map opposite page

Description: Two 200-yard-long trails lead to overlooks at the rim of a steep canyon offering spectacular views of Deep Creek, 2,300 feet below. Douglas-fir grows along the moist creek bottom, with south-facing slopes of piñon and juniper. Surrounding mesas are blanketed with wildflowers from early July through August. The trail to the west of the parking lot has been developed for universal-access. Limber pines next to the parking lot are estimated to be 700 years old. www.fs.fed.us

Viewing information: Around the parking lot and overlooks watch for golden-mantled ground squirrels, marmots, and least chipmunks. A variety of raptors are visible from the overlook. Scan the canyon rim during summer and fall for herds of elk. At dusk bats can be seen at the canyon rim, including Yuma, long-legged, long-eared, and little brown myotis. Early fall you may see bats swarming, a unique event in this part of Colorado. In evening watch and listen for great horned, long-eared, and saw-whet owls. Long-eared owls have been seen here. Fee for camping.

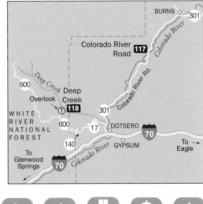

Ownership: USFS (970-328-6388)

Size: One acre

Closest town: Gypsum, 26 miles; lodging, restaurants

Directions: See map this page

This myotis, or mouse-eared, bat flies with its mouth open as it echolocates, emitting a stream of ultra-high-pitched sounds, then reading the echoes as the calls bounce back from prey. A colony of a quarter million bats can eat 20 tons of insects in one night. CLAUDE STEELMAN

Description: This spectacular, steep, rock-walled canyon was carved by the Colorado River. Habitats vary along the route, including rocky slopes with scattered trees and shrubs, grassy meadows, riverside riparian woodlands, and wetlands of willow and sedges, with spruce-fir forest on mountainsides. The paved walking and biking trail travels from the west end of Glenwood Springs to Dotsero.

Viewing information: Wildlife is most visible in the eastern third and western third of the canyon. The central third is too steep and deep for much wildlife. Black bears may be seen through much of the canyon, mostly on the south side. Bighorn sheep can generally be spotted downstream from the power plant on the north side of the canyon. Look also for deer and elk. Mountain lions may be seen in areas inhabited by deer. Be sure to look up into the canyon's deep air spaces for red-tailed hawks, golden eagles, white-throated swifts, peregrine falcons (south side of the canyon, east of the big tunnel). Listen for canyon wrens. Beavers, mink, ringtails, coyotes. Around October 10, Grizzly Creek is thick with spawning mountain whitefish, which are easily viewed in the shallow water. The last-completed section of Interstate 70, constructed with conservation of the canyon's scenic and natural values in mind, passes through the canyon. Interpretive exhibits at rest areas and at either end of the trail. High water and snow may close the trail. Call CDOT for trail conditions. Contact CDOW (970-947-2920) for information on wildlife.

Ownership: CDOT (970-945-3840)

Size: 18.7 miles

Closest town: Glenwood Springs, 1 mile; lodging, restaurants; Dotsero

Directions: *See map opposite page*

Mountain lions, also called pumas or cougars, are sighted more frequently in Colorado as people increasingly move into lion country. W. PERRY CONWAY

Description: Formed when the rest of the lake dropped to the floor of the canyon and "left it hanging," Hanging Lake sits suspended in a 500-foot bowl on the steep east wall of Deadhorse Canyon, a side canyon of Glenwood Canyon. Waterfalls spilling down the canyon wall feed the lake. Mineral deposits in the water give the lake its green color. A wooden boardwalk rims the lake. Spectacular scenic site, but the 1.5-mile trail to the lake through spruce/fir forest is **steep**. Hanging Lake can only be accessed from the eastbound lanes of Interstate 70, exit 125. Westbound travelers must exit at Grizzly Creek (exit 121) and follow the signs east to exit 125.

Viewing information: Watch for black and white-throated swifts feeding above the lake. The black swifts nest behind the waterfalls. Best place to watch birds is from the boardwalk. Good trout viewing from the boardwalk into the clear water. Watch for other mountain wildlife such as Clark's nutcrackers, gray jays, tree and violet-green swallows, chipmunks, and golden-mantled ground squirrels.

Ownership: USFS (970-328-6388)

Size: 15 acres

Closest town: Glenwood Springs, 10 miles; restaurants, lodging

Directions: See map this page

ROCKY MOUNTAINS

Hanging Lake is easily accessible from a parking lot off Interstate 70. The lake east of Glenwood Springs offers scenic beauty and abundant wildlife. DAN PEHA

Description: The Fryingpan River Road (begins as County Road 104 and changes to Forest Road 105), follows the Fryingpan River from its confluence with the Roaring Fork River at Basalt to its headwaters. As it climbs in elevation the road passes through piñon-juniper woodlands, lodgepole, aspen, and Douglas-fir forests to the open water of Ruedi Reservoir at an altitude of 10,000 feet. The road continues 30 miles beyond the dam to alpine tundra habitat around Hagerman Pass, then on to the town of Leadville. **Call ahead to check if the pass is open.**

Viewing information: The first 14 miles of the road offer prime winter wildlife viewing. Bald eagles are common, especially at the catch-and-release fishing area just below Ruedi Dam. All age classes of eagles can be seen. The Fryingpan River is a world-class trout fishery, especially the two miles below the dam. Lake, brown, rainbow, brook, and some cutthroat trout and kokanee salmon in Ruedi Reservoir. Watch for golden eagles, kingfishers, green-winged teal, goldeneyes, and other birds. Deer and elk are often seen on hillsides above the river in mornings and evenings. Watch for bighorn sheep grazing along the road on most days. The ranger district office in Carbondale offers interpretive exhibits, an on-site naturalist, publications, and checklists.

Ownership: USFS, Eagle County, Pitkin County, PVT (Basalt Chamber of Commerce, 970-927-4031)

Size: 14 miles   **Closest town:** Basalt; lodging, restaurants

Directions: See map opposite page

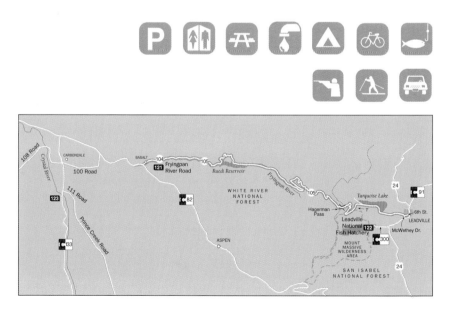

122. LEADVILLE NATIONAL FISH HATCHERY

Description: This historic hatchery building, built in 1889 out of native red sandstone, is on the National Register of Historic Places. Second oldest fish hatchery in U.S. Fish are raised in cement raceways. There is a display pond of fish. Lodgepole pine forest surrounds the hatchery. **www.leadville.fws.gov**

Viewing information: View trout and eggs (in December) being raised in a hatchery operation. Visitor center in historic hatchery building offers interpretive exhibits. Reservations required for guided tours—eight-person minimum—but interpretive hosts are on site during summer to answer questions. Visitors can feed trout in summer. Groups can reserve Evergreen Lake picnic area. Hiking, wildlife viewing, and catch-and-release fishing for native greenback cutthroat trout in adjacent Mount Massive Wilderness Area. One mile nature trail.

Ownership: USFWS (719-486-0189)

Size: 3,057 acres   **Closest town:** Leadville, 6 miles; lodging, restaurants

Directions: See map opposite page

123. CRYSTAL RIVER HATCHERY

Description: Located in the heart of the Crystal River Valley, at the foot of Mount Sopris. The hatchery building houses the incubation and hatching facilities for trout eggs collected by hand from fish in the outdoor raceways. Annually, 11 million eggs are collected and sent to other hatcheries to be reared for release for sport fishing. Hatchery-reared eggs have a 95% survival rate compared with less than 0.3% in the wild. **www.wildlife.state.co.us**

Viewing information: Excellent viewing of Snake River cutthroat and rainbow trout in raceways, open daytime for self-guided tours. Guided/group tours need reservations. September through January, visitors can observe all spawning and hatching operations, upon request. Visitors encouraged to feed fish. Good wildlife viewing around hatchery. Bald eagles (winter), waterfowl, osprey (migration) on river and nearby pond. Songbirds, owls, herons, kingfishers along river and in riparian woodlands. Mammals include deer, beavers, muskrats, coyotes, raccoons, bears and skunks.

Ownership: CDOW (970-963-2665)   **Size:** 19 acres

Closest town: Carbondale, 1 mile north, restaurants, lodging

Directions: See map opposite page

Description: This driving tour begins in the open mountain valley called South Park and goes over a timberline pass of the Mosquito Range, passing through a variety of habitats. Open sagebrush grasslands of South Park, riparian habitats along the South Fork of the South Platte River and tributary streams, a wetland below a man-made lake, high-elevation forests with stands of aspen, alpine tundra around the summit. **www.fs.fed.us**

Viewing information: Excellent auto tour for elk and raptors. Watch for pronghorn in open areas as you drive through South Park. Eleven miles south of Fairplay, County Road 22 leads west along the South Fork of the South Platte River. On the right, search in spring for ibis, avocets, and phalaropes in a wetland on private property (watch from the road). In winter, watch for elk along the first eight miles of the road. Check fencelines for shrikes, bluebirds, kingbirds. Bears are sometimes seen. Riparian habitats along the streams are good for warblers, finches, sparrows. As the road climbs, bighorn sheep may be seen on rocky precipices. A trailhead at Rich Creek leads to a high-elevation basin with huge herds of elk in summer. Wild turkeys and mountain lions are sometimes seen. Below the summit of Weston Pass watch for golden eagles, harriers, goshawks, red-tailed hawks, merlins. Bighorn sheep may be spotted on Weston Peak to the north. You can continue on the route down to Leadville, though wildlife viewing is not as good on this drier west side. Watch for beavers along Big Union Creek. **High clearance vehicle is needed.**

Ownership: USFS (719-836-2031), PVT

Size: 25-mile drive

Closest town: Fairplay, 12 miles; Leadville,14 miles; lodging, restaurants

Directions: *See map this page*

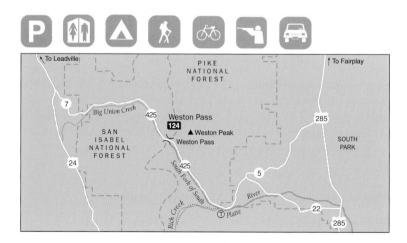

125. ASPEN CENTER FOR ENVIRONMENTAL STUDIES (ACES)

Description: This interpretive and educational facility located at the Hallam Lake Nature Preserve in the town of Aspen includes a 25-acre preserve along the Roaring Fork River. A short boardwalk loop trail, with other trails spiraling off, overlooks wetlands and riparian habitat. **www.aspennature.org**

Viewing information: Waterfowl is abundant. Watch for beavers and muskrats on the pond. A great variety of birds inhabit the riparian areas. Also watch for hawks, owls, deer, foxes, bears. Guided tours off-site four times a day and special tours by arrangement. Self-guided tours and nature walks, field study and environmental education programs for local schools, summer naturalist programs, snowshoe tours, evening lectures, birds of prey programs. Open Monday through Friday year-round, Saturdays in spring, summer, and fall.

Ownership: ACES (970-925-5756)

Size: 25 acres

Closest town: Aspen, in town; lodging, restaurants

Directions: *See map this page*

126. MAROON LAKE

Description: Mix of habitats from mountain forest to high-elevation forest, open water, mountain meadows, mountain stream, and willow communities at and above the lake. Alpine tundra accessible from hiking trails. Mixed forest of subalpine fir-Engelmann spruce surround the lake. **www.fs.fed.us**

Viewing information: Mule deer, elk, and bighorn sheep seen frequently. Also watch ridgelines and bowls to the east of the road for elk. Bald eagles in winter and spring; smaller birds abundant. Check the creek for dippers. Wildlife viewing area with spotting scopes and interpretive signs near the West Maroon Portal. In summer the road to Maroon Lake is closed to passenger cars from 9 a.m. to 5 p.m. Visitors may take a public bus to the Lake and points between. Visit website or call ranger district for current rules, schedules and fee information. Interpretive exhibits, on-site naturalist, available at the Aspen Ranger District office.

Ownership: USFS (970-935-3445)

Size: 5 miles of road

Closest town: Aspen, 3 miles; loding, restaurants   **Directions:** *See map this page*

Description: A 38-mile drive across a spectacular mountain pass traversing several ecosystems including aspen and spruce-fir forests, willow riparian communities, mountain meadows, mountain shrublands, and alpine tundra. The pass summit lies above timberline at 12,095 feet. Highway pullouts, summit parking lot, campgrounds, and hiking trailheads offer access for wildlife viewing and hiking. Scenic views and mid-summer wildflowers are outstanding. Check road conditions with Colorado Dept. of Transportation in winter. www.fs.fed.us

Viewing information: Mule deer, elk, and an occasional black bear can be seen along the road. Birds are abundant. Aspen forests attract a variety of nesting birds such as western wood pewees, warbling vireos, flickers, downy woodpeckers. Look for willow flycatchers; yellow and Wilson's warblers; white-crowned, song, and fox sparrows in willow riparian areas; golden-crowned and ruby-crowned kinglets; olive-sided flycatchers; brown creepers; hairy woodpeckers; red-naped sapsuckers; goshawks; hermit thrushes in spruce-fir forest; and pipits, horned larks, and white-tailed ptarmigan on the alpine tundra. Above timberline watch also for pikas, marmots, mountain goats, red-tailed hawks. Look for beavers along the north fork of Lake Creek. The road is closed to vehicles in winter but open to snowmobiles and cross-country skiing.

Ownership: USFS (970-925-3445)

Size: 38-mile drive

Closest town: Twin Lakes, 2 miles; Aspen, 2 miles; lodging, restaurants

Directions: *See map this page*

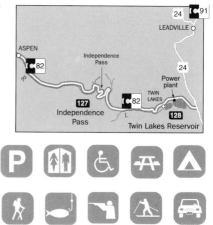

Mule deer, the most common deer in Colorado, are found statewide, from the alpine tundra to the eastern plains, and in almost every habitat in the state. NEAL AND MJ MISHLER

Description: Located at an elevation of 9,000 feet, this reservoir is surrounded by high-elevation forest with small patches of aspen and lodgepole pine. Alpine habitat visible on surrounding high peaks. The Forest Service burns and irrigates the wetland at the west end of the reservoir to benefit a very large wintering elk herd. The wetland has thick willows, sedges, and grass. Seasonal flooding produces wet meadows. There are two beaver ponds along the highway boundary. The south Mount Elbert trail to Colorado's highest peak, which lies about five miles to the northwest, begins near the power plant open summer months. The Colorado Trail traverses about three-quarters of the lake border. www.recreation.gov

Viewing information: Good wildlife viewing along the south side of the reservoir. Winter is a good time to see abundant elk and deer in the valley bottom. Check the wetlands west of the reservoir for beavers and muskrats. In spring and summer watch for red-winged blackbirds, white-crowned sparrows, yellow warblers, and other songbirds in willows and wetland areas. In spring watch for cinnamon and blue-winged teal, western and eared grebes, white-faced ibis. Raptors include red-tailed hawks, goshawks, and ospreys (summer). Alpine species, including ptarmigan and marmots, are observable at various times of year. Good viewing of the lake and some of the wetland at the power plant along Colorado Highway 82 on the north side of the reservoir. The Mount Elbert Visitor Center, at the power plant, open summer months, offers interpretive exhibits and information. The road around the west side between the town of Twin Lakes and the gauging station is closed from late November to May to protect elk on their winter range and during calving season.

Ownership: USFS (719-486-0749), BOR

Size: 7,000 acres   **Closest town:** Twin Lakes, two miles; lodging, restaurants

***Directions:** See map opposite page*

Aspen groves create an open canopy which enables sunlight to penetrate to the forest floor and encourage extensive plant growth. The diverse plant life in these groves provides food and shelter for hundreds of wildlife species, including elk.
SHERM SPOELSTRA

ROCKY MOUNTAINS

129. HECKENDORF STATE WILDLIFE AREA

Description: Located in foothills at the base of the Sawatch Range, this site lies in an alluvial fan of the Arkansas River. The high mountains of the Collegiate Peaks offer a scenic backdrop to uplands of sagebrush and grasses. Stands of ponderosa pine at the west end of the property and piñon-juniper at the drier east end. www.wildlife.state.co.us

Viewing information: Elk viewing very good December to April. Watch also for mule deer and pronghorn. A variety of raptors may be seen including prairie falcons, kestrels, golden eagles, red-tailed and rough-legged hawks. Mountain plovers, considered a bird of the shortgrass prairie of eastern Colorado, have been discovered nesting in this high mountain park. Other mammals to watch for include thirteen-lined and Wyoming ground squirrels, coyotes, jackrabbits, cottontails, badgers. A wildlife viewing platform is planned.

Ownership: CDOW (719-530-5520)

Size: 640 acres

Closest town: Buena Vista, 5 miles; lodging, restaurants

Directions: *See map opposite page*

130. LOVE RANCH

Description: A lush, 11-acre hay meadow at the foot of the steep, rocky Chalk Cliffs on Mount Princeton. Cottonwoods, alder, birch, and chokecherry along Chalk Creek. An irrigation ditch runs along the meadow. www.cwhf.org

Viewing information: A ground-level viewing deck overlooks a hay meadow that is used by bighorn sheep year-round, though best viewing is December through May. The animals are generally visible 100 feet to 200 yards away. Watch for mountain goats on the Chalk Cliffs, especially in winter. Elk seen in the meadow occasionally. Year-round watch for mule deer, coyotes, cottontails, short-tailed weasels, golden-mantled ground squirrels, and Gunnison's prairie dogs. Golden eagles and a variety of raptors are visible around the cliffs in all seasons. Viewing kiosk with interpretive panels describing area history and wildlife.

Ownership: Colorado Wildlife Heritage Foundation (303-291-7212)

Size: 11 acres

Closest town: Nathrop, 8 miles

Directions: *See map opposite page*

Description: The lake lies in a narrow canyon along Cottonwood Creek as a side trip on the route from Buena Vista over Cottonwood Pass. The south side of the canyon is steep and heavily forested, with spruce fir and aspen right down to the water. The inlet on the west is filled with thick willows and bulrushes. The north side along the road is a strip of wild rose, grasses, and forbs at the foot of steep cliffs. **www.fs.fed.us**

Viewing information: Mountain goats can be seen on the cliffs that start at the junction of the Cottonwood Pass road and the Cottonwood Lake road, and taper out just past the lake. Viewers should pull off the road and view from the pullouts on the way to the lake. Check the interpretive sign at the lake's west end for information about goats in general. From the exhibit watch for goats by looking northeast at the cliffs. Golden-mantled ground squirrels and chipmunks are common on dry, rocky slopes. Watch for deer and elk at the west side of the lake and check out the beaver ponds. Abundant beaver activity below the lake. Watch for waterfowl like blue-winged teal and mallards on the water. Surrounding forests are home to mountain birds such as gray and Steller's jays, yellow-rumped warblers, dark-eyed juncos, pine siskins. Continue over Cottonwood Pass at 12,126 feet for good high-elevation forest and alpine viewing.

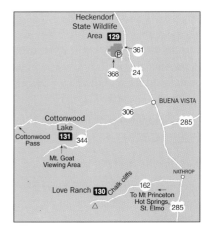

Ownership: USFS (719-539-3591)

Size: 4,500 acres

Closest town: Buena Vista, 10 miles; lodging, restaurants

Directions: See map this page

Mountain goats were not known to inhabit Colorado in recent history. They were released in the state in the 1940s and several populations of goats are now well established in the Colorado mountains.
M.H. LEVY

ROCKY MOUNTAINS

139

Description: This river trip along the Arkansas River, part of the Arkansas Headwaters Recreation Area, begins at Fisherman's Bridge Recreation Site and continues 10 miles downstream through Browns Canyon to the Hecla Junction Recreation Site. Dry, rocky canyon sides are dominated by piñon pine, juniper, and scattered ponderosa mixed with shrublands. Browns Canyon is a technical boating run with **class IV whitewater rapids** and should only be attempted by experienced private boaters or with one of 63 permitted commercial outfitters. Water flows best in summer. **Road 194 is not maintained November through April**. www.parks.state.co.us

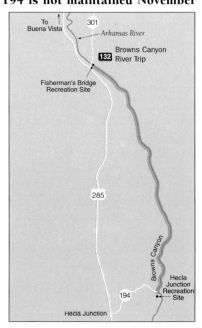

Viewing information: Watch for bighorn sheep on rocky outcrops year-round. Mule deer abundant. Beavers, coyotes, and gray foxes sometimes visible along the shore. A variety of waterfowl and songbirds can be seen. Also watch for great blue herons, bald and golden eagles, turkey vultures, and peregrine falcons. Black bears, mountain lions, and bobcats inhabit the canyon but are rarely seen.

Ownership: State Parks (719-539-7289), BLM

Size: 10 miles along the river

Closest town: Buena Vista, 15 miles; lodging, restaurants

Directions: *See map this page*

Bobcats are found statewide and in many habitats, though they are most common in rough country of piñon pine and juniper. They have smaller paws and are more spotted than the closely related lynx.
MACK AND SHARON JOHNSON

Description: The "triangle" is bordered by the Taylor and East Rivers and Jacks Cabin Cutoff Road/Forest Road 813. It is a sagebrush, aspen, and mixed conifer wintering range for bighorn sheep, mule deer, and elk. Prime viewing areas are marked by signs and parking. Local botanists favor this area in late May and June for the large diversity of wildflowers found there just after the snow has melted and for the outstanding views of the East River Valley.

Viewing information: From late November through April, watch for bighorn sheep on south- and east-facing slopes on the southern edge of the triangle and in the Taylor River Canyon. Deer are most visible along the East River, with elk sighted everywhere. To protect the animals, **the area is closed to public access and all human activity December 1 through April 1,** when viewing must be done from the highway. Some bighorn sheep are visible in summer.

Ownership: City of Gunnison, USFS (970-641-0471)

Size: 9 square miles

Closest town: Almont; restaurants, lodging

Directions: *See map this page*

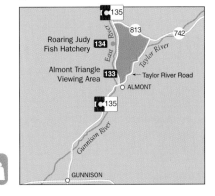

Description: The hatchery is located in a wide valley along the East River. Sagebrush hillsides above low-lying grassy meadows with willow thickets and cottonwood riparian areas along the river. Numerous springs provide year-round water. The hatchery is open seven days a week. Call for current hours. **www.wildlife.state.co.us**

Viewing information: Lots of shore and songbirds in the marshy willow bottoms and wet meadows. In winter, watch for bald eagles along the river. Osprey are occasionally sighted. Kokanee salmon are spawned in the hatchery from late October to early November. Visitors can view the milking and fertilization of eggs. Call the hatchery for viewing times. Young salmon and cutthroat and rainbow trout can be viewed in ponds and raceways at the hatchery.

Ownership: CDOW (970-641-0190)   **Size:** 776 acres

Closest town: Almont, 5 miles; restaurants, lodging

Directions: *See map above*

ROCKY MOUNTAINS

Description: This driving tour follows Hot Springs Creek, a flowing stream lined with mature mountain riparian habitat of cottonwoods and willows, surrounded by drier sagebrush uplands on the back side of Tomichi Dome. Large sagebrush basin at Waunita Hot Springs is interspersed with conifers and stands of aspen. Tour route passes over Waunita Pass then along Quartz Creek through mixed aspen and coniferous forest into high-elevation forest and meadows at Cumberland Pass and down into large, open sagebrush basin of Taylor Park. Several lakes and, above timberline, talus slopes with lingering snow fields. **Roads 763 and 765 are not maintained for winter travel.** www.fs.fed.us

Viewing information: Mule deer and elk common year-round. Lots of beaver activity—lodges, dams, pools—along Hot Springs, Quartz, and Willow creeks. Good chance to view fish in pools and streams. Fishing pond for small children at the USFS campground outside Pitkin offers good viewing of stocked trout. Watch in sagebrush habitat for Gunnison sage grouse. dusky grouse at higher elevations. Some mallards and waterfowl use the beaver ponds. Services available only seasonally at Pitkin and Tincup.

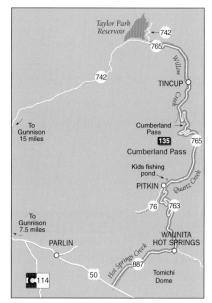

Ownership: USFS (970-641-0471)

Size: 35 miles, one way

Closest town: Gunnison, 32 miles; lodging, restaurants

Directions: See map this page

Rainbow trout are raised in Colorado fish hatcheries and released into state rivers and lakes to supplement native fisheries.
KEN ARCHER

Description: Sagebrush hillsides surround irrigated hay meadows, with cottonwood/willow riparian areas along the Beaver Creek drainage. The parking lot overlooks the valley bottom where elk and deer feed in winter. The CDOW is planting shrubs near the duck ponds to increase forage. There are interpretive signs at the overlook, and a 0.25-mile interpretive trail follows the ridge south from the viewing area. Six new waterfowl ponds have been built in the meadow for shorebirds. **www.wildlife.state.co.us**

Viewing information: The valley is important winter range for deer and elk. They are visible feeding in the meadow and on hillsides from late December to early March. In spring and summer, songbird viewing along Beaver Creek is good.

Ownership: CDOW (970-641-7060), BLM

Size: 2,800 acres   **Closest town:** Gunnison, 6.25 miles; restaurants, lodging

Directions: See map below

137. GUNNISON SAGE GROUSE MATING GROUND

Description: Irrigated hay meadow on private land. Flat, open terrain. Adjacent riparian habitat to the east. Viewing site is a pullout on a gravel county road.

Viewing information: This site is a communal mating ground, or lek, for Gunnison sage grouse. The birds gather early in the morning in spring and the male grouse display to attract mates. Viewing is from the second week of April through the first week of May. Visitors should arrive before dawn. Observation site is 200 to 400 yards west of the mating ground. Binoculars or spotting scope needed for good viewing. **Visitors may leave their cars but must remain at the road pullout and not enter the meadow, which is private property.** Interpretive sign explains sage grouse mating behavior.

Ownership: CDOW (970-641-7060, or BLM 970-641-0471), PVT

Size: N/A   **Closest town:** Gunnison, 17 miles; restaurants, lodging

Directions: See map this page

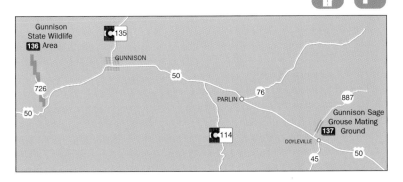

ROCKY MOUNTAINS

Description: A variety of habitats surround this reservoir along the Gunnison River, part of the Curecanti National Recreation Area. Above the reservoir are grasslands and riparian areas. Mosaics of mountain shrublands mixed with high-desert sagebrush line the lakeshore. Side canyons host mixed stands of Douglas-fir and aspen. Open water of the lake extends into secluded lake arms. **www.nps.gov**

Viewing information: Watch for a variety of songbirds in riparian areas spring through fall. Abundant waterfowl on the lake, particularly during migration. Good viewing of deer, elk, and bald and golden eagles in winter. A herd of 20 bighorn sheep inhabits the Dillon Pinnacles area. Check the middle bridge area across the reservoir, and north of the reservoir along U.S. Highway 50 for sheep, as well as around Dillon Mesa. When boating, scan slopes north of the lake for sheep. **Sapinero State Wildlife Area**, on the north side of the reservoir, offers good access to habitat for wildlife viewing and hiking. Habitat stamp required to use state wildlife area.

Ownership: NPS (970-641-2337), BOR, CDOW

Size: 30,000 acres

Closest town: Gunnison, 10 miles; lodging, restaurants

Directions: See map this page

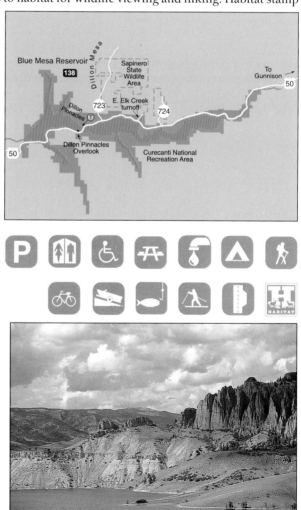

Blue Mesa Reservoir is the largest body of water in the state. The rocky Dillon Pinnacles is a good place to spot bighorn sheep.
TIM CRISMAN

Description: A mosaic of open grasslands with Douglas-fir and ponderosa pine in draws and arroyos. Some aspen stands, with mountain shrubs on hillsides. Riparian zones of alder. Fairly sheer cliffs on the south and southwest offer good raptor nesting. Good road system. **County road access is by four-wheel-drive vehicle only. Restrictions prohibit vehicle use from March 15 to May 15 due to wet conditions.** www.blm.gov

Viewing information: Trickle Mountain features Colorado's four major hoofed species—pronghorn, mule deer, elk, and bighorn sheep—all using the same habitat. Golden eagles and prairie falcons nest in cliffs. Rough-legged hawks frequent the area and peregrine falcons are occasionally sighted. Management site for Rio Grande cutthroat trout. Look for beaver ponds on Tuttle Creek.

Ownership: BLM (719-655-2547)

Size: 53,000 acres

Closest town: Saguache, 11.25 miles; restaurants, lodging

Directions: See map this page

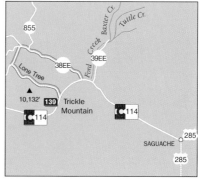

This mule deer buck will shed its antlers in the winter and begin growing another set in the spring. The animal was named for its large, mulelike ears.
DENNIS HENRY

Description: Large wetland complex with many marshes and small, shallow lakes providing excellent habitat for migratory waterfowl, wading birds, and shorebirds. Located among dry shrublands of the San Luis Valley. Portions are closed to public access during waterfowl and shorebird nesting periods, February 15 to July 15. Binoculars are necessary. Winter viewing opportunities are limited. Interpretive signs, trail, and boardwalk. The nature trail is open year-round during daylight hours. www.wildlife.state.co.us

Viewing information: Because the water source is primarily artesian wells, viewing opportunities are nearly year-round for waterfowl, wading birds, and shorebirds. Excellent opportunities to see white-faced ibis, snowy egrets, and white pelicans, as well as a wide variety of songbirds. Nesting avocets, spotted sandpipers, Wilson's phalaropes, and black terns. Watch for shorebirds in ditches along the county roads.

Ownership: BOR, CDOW (719-587-6900)

Size: 5,433 acres

Closest town: Saguache, 12.5 miles; restaurants, lodging

Directions: *See map this page*

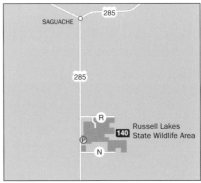

This female Wilson's phalarope is more colorful and larger than her mate. The birds spin top-like in the water and feed on insects sucked into the resulting whirlpool. KEN ARCHER

Water attracts many varieties of birds to the Russell Lakes State Wildlife Area in southern Colorado's San Luis Valley. BOB HERNBRODE

Description: Located within the Summer Coon Volcano, the Natural Arch is a wall of volcanic rock with a window through it. Surrounding terrain combines rolling piñon-juniper woodlands with open grasslands. This driving tour begins in Del Norte. Follow Colorado Highway 112 north for one mile, then turn west on a paved road toward the airport. After crossing the canal, turn left on County Road 15 north, to FR 660. Stay right and follow this to the turnoff for Natural Arch. The Arch includes remarkable geologic formations. Travel 0.5 mile past the turnoff and turn left onto a two-track road. Follow this to interpretive signs at the base of Eagle Rock. To complete the circle, retrace your route to FR 660, then head east to the stop sign at the gravel county road. Turn right (south) until you reach CO 112. Return south to Del Norte. www.fs.fed.us www.blm.gov

Viewing information: Watch for pronghorn as you drive into the area. Elk are visible in the area in winter; mule deer, bighorn sheep, and pronghorn can be seen year-round. From the road you may see loggerhead shrikes, horned larks, vesper and Brewer's sparrows. In the area of Eagle Rock, watch for mountain bluebirds, pinyon jays, green-tailed towhees, bushtits, various flycatchers, and sparrows. Scan the ledges of Eagle Rock for bighorn sheep; best viewing before mid-morning. Eagle Rock, and surrounding airspace, host prairie and peregrine falcons, ravens, rock wrens, and white-throated swifts.

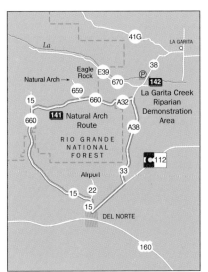

Ownership: BLM, PVT, USFS (719-657-3321)

Size: 100 acres

Closest town: Del Norte, 5 miles; restaurants, lodging

Directions: *See map this page*

Wildflowers dot meadows along the route of the Natural Arch Watchable Wildlife Area. TIM CRISMAN

142. LA GARITA CREEK RIPARIAN DEMONSTRATION AREA

Description: Cottonwood/alder/willow riparian zones along the creek surrounded by wet meadows and pastureland. Located where the creek flows out of the mountains onto the valley floor. The area is being managed to improve water quality and fish habitat, stabilize banks, and improve riparian vegetation to serve as an example of what can be done to manage riparian sites. www.blm.gov

Viewing information: An excellent area for viewing migratory and nesting songbirds: orioles, thrushes, towhees, vireos, wrens, warblers, chickadees, sparrows, woodpeckers, and juncos. Good site for great horned owls. Great blue herons use sandy flats along the creek. Elk, mule deer, and pronghorn can be sighted along Colorado Highway 112 and County Road 33 to La Garita.

Ownership: BLM (719-655-2547)

Size: 1,375 acres

Closest town: Del Norte, 10.5 miles; restaurants, lodging

Directions: *See map previous page*

See map previous page

Dark-eyed juncos forage on the ground for seeds and insects. The birds often nest in small, well-concealed ground impressions. WELDON LEE

ROCKY MOUNTAINS

Description: The national park is a fascinating geological site with sand dunes up to 700 feet high at the base of the Sangre de Cristo range. Surrounding habitats include rabbitbrush shrublands and piñon-juniper woodlands. Scattered ponderosa pine, a few aspen groves and cottonwood riparian areas border Medano and Mosca creeks, as well as other intermittent waterways through the monument. Inquire at the visitor center for information. There are 15 miles of trails in the park—0.5 nature trail and guided nature walks. www.nps.gov

Viewing information: Mule deer are visible everywhere, and elk are sometimes seen in winter near the entrance. Pronghorn can be seen on the approach to the monument, and bighorn sheep are visible along the road to Medano Pass (requires four-wheel-drive vehicle). Six species of endemic insects inhabit the sand dunes. Kangaroo rats are everywhere at night; watch for their holes in vegetated upland areas of the dunes. Other mammals include chipmunks, rock and golden-mantled ground squirrels, desert and Nuttall's cottontails, coyotes, bobcats, mountain lions, and black bears. Animal tracks are visible on the dunes in early morning. Good songbird viewing in wooded areas. Species include magpies, mountain bluebirds, western tanagers, chickadees, flickers, nutcrackers, grosbeaks, white-throated swifts, green-tailed towhees, and nighthawks; scrub, pinyon, and Steller's jays; Lewis's and downy woodpeckers; and broad-tailed and rufous hummingbirds. Fantastic view from nearby scenic **Zapata Falls** offers a good place to see elk and songbirds, particularly spring through fall. Reaching the falls requires wading in a creek.

Ownership: NPS (719-378-2312), BLM

Size: 38,659 acres

Closest town: Mosca, 19 miles; restaurants, lodging

Directions: *See map below*

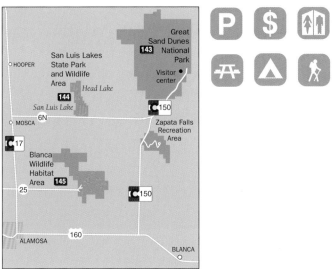

144. SAN LUIS LAKES STATE PARK AND WILDLIFE AREA

Description: Shrubland of salt grass, greasewood, and rabbitbrush surrounds Head and San Luis lakes. Sedge/bulrush wet meadows in low-lying areas between the lakes. The area is fed by intermittent water from springs and creeks; very wet during spring runoff. The southern one-third of the area is a state park. Portions are closed to public access during waterfowl and shorebird nesting periods, February 15 to July 15. Look for the Colorado rare plant, slender spiderflower, at the edges of alkali wetlands. **www.parks.state.co.us**

Viewing information: Many resident Canada geese and dabbling ducks, especially mallards, pintails, and gadwalls. Good potential for seeing concentrations of canvasbacks and occasional mergansers on San Luis Lake. During summer watch for eared, western, and Clark's grebes, ruddy ducks, black-crowned night herons. Also white pelicans and herons on the lakes; bitterns and snipes in the meadows. Raptors include prairie and peregrine falcons, bald eagles, northern harriers, great horned owls. Sage thrashers are common.

Ownership: CDOW, SLB, State Parks (719-378-2020)

Size: 2,954 acres   **Closest town:** Mosca, 7.5 miles; restaurants, lodging

Directions: See map opposite page

145. BLANCA WILDLIFE HABITAT AREA

Description: Large acreage on the floor of the San Luis Valley below 14,345-foot Blanca Peak consists of old lake beds edged by sand dunes. Earthen dikes and artesian wells have created a series of ponds as waterfowl nesting habitat. Some ponds have cattail/bulrush marshes; others offer wild plum and cottonwoods to encourage various wildlife species. Portions are closed to public access during waterfowl and shorebird nesting periods, February 15 to July 15. Biting insects are severe in July and August. **www.blm.gov**

Viewing information: Excellent duck viewing. Shore, wading, and marsh birds include avocets, black-crowned night herons, several species of sandpipers, snowy plovers, white pelicans, and red-winged and yellow-headed blackbirds. During fall migration, concentrations of sandpipers and Wilson's phalaropes can reach the thousands. Peak time is August 15 to September 15. Waterflow designed to keep some ponds ice-free in winter, attracting bald eagles. BLM has erected eagle roosts. Good viewing of hawks, as well as northern harriers. Mammals include muskrats, cottontails, foxes, and coyotes.

Ownership: BLM (719-274-8971) **Size:** 9,850 acres

Closest town: Alamosa, 12.5 miles; restaurants, lodging

Directions: See map opposite page

Description: An area of developed ponds and wetlands managed for waterfowl along the Rio Grande River. Thick cottonwood/willow communities in bottomlands along the river channel. Artesian wells feed warm-water ponds surrounded by scattered cottonwoods. **Area closed to public access during waterfowl and shorebird nesting, February 15 to July 15.** www.wildlife.state.co.us

Viewing information: Excellent viewing of resident waterfowl. Many dabbling ducks (mallards, gadwalls, pintails) and Canada geese. Look for diving ducks on the bigger ponds, especially ruddy ducks and goldeneyes. Some sandhill cranes in spring and fall. Occasional great blue herons, night-herons, white-faced ibis, and bitterns in marshy areas. Good area for cavity-nesting songbirds in wooded areas—swallows, woodpeckers, and creepers—and warblers among the willows. Raptors include great horned owls, northern harriers, Swainson's and ferruginous hawks, and bald eagles (in winter). Numerous beavers, muskrats, and mule deer.

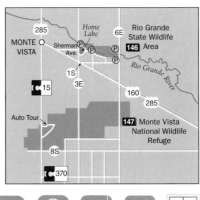

Ownership: CDOW (719-587-6900)

Size: 1,450 acres

Closest town: Monte Vista, 3.5 miles; restaurants, lodging

Directions: See map this page

No wonder more animals can be found in the riparian areas—there is more water, food, and cover for them there.

Description: Located in the arid San Luis Valley, the refuge is a complex of ponds and marshes created and managed to provide nesting and feeding habitat for waterfowl and other wildlife. By contrast, surrounding greasewood uplands are dry. Farmed plots of grain and alfalfa supplement natural food sources. www.fws.gov

Viewing information: Throughout March the refuge and surrounding fields are an important staging ground for greater sandhill cranes. Look for a few whooping cranes in the sandhill flock. Thousands of cranes return in October and stay four to eight weeks. Twenty species of ducks, four species of geese, swans, snipe, sandpipers, herons, egrets, white-faced ibis have been sighted here. Numerous songbirds nest or migrate through. Watch for short-eared owls. Fall duck populations can exceed 35,000. Bald eagles visible in winter. A bird list is available. Mammals include mule deer, elk, muskrats, rabbits, and coyotes. Clumps of cottonwoods scattered throughout the refuge offer opportunities to see warblers, flycatchers, woodpeckers, great horned owls in summer and during spring and fall migration. The self-guided auto tour route is open dawn to dusk year-round. Headquarters is at Alamosa National Wildlife Refuge, site 148 (next page).

Ownership: USFWS (719-589-4021)

Size: 14,189 acres

Closest town: Monte Vista, 6.25 miles; restaurants, lodging

Directions: See map opposite page

ROCKY MOUNTAINS

During spring and fall migrations, large concentrations of waterfowl stop over at Monte Vista National Wildlife Refuge in the San Luis Valley. D. ROBERT FRANZ

Description: A complex of river oxbows, pools, wet meadows, and cottonwood/willow riparian habitats within the flood plain of the Rio Grande River. Drier upland habitats and agricultural fields surround the refuge. **www.fws.gov**

Viewing information: An 80-foot-high bluff overlooking the Refuge is a good place to spot up to 100 bald eagles in winter and early spring feeding on winter-killed fish. Watch also for an abundance of waterfowl and wading birds, golden eagles, great horned and short-eared owls, and other raptors. Sandhill cranes are abundant in the area in March and October and many roost on the refuge. A two-mile trail follows the river. Excellent birdwatching for various warblers, woodpeckers, flycatchers, and other nesting and migratory birds, including such unusual migrants as indigo buntings and blue grosbeaks. A self-guided auto tour gives good viewing of wetland species. Refuge headquarters is open Monday through Friday and offers interpretive exhibits and checklists. Public should call for hours.

Ownership: USFWS (719-589-4021)

Size: 11,169 acres

Closest town: Alamosa, 5 miles; restaurants, lodging

Directions: *See map this page*

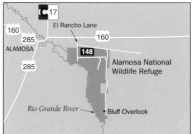

Some 20,000 sandhill cranes gather in the San Luis Valley in March as they migrate north to nest. You can't miss their croaking calls as hundreds of birds feed in fields or pass overhead. WENDY SHATTIL/BOB ROZINSKI

Description: La Jara Creek flows through a narrow, rocky canyon with willows and cottonwoods along it, some meadows, and piñon-juniper woodlands on uplands. The smaller Hot Creek flows through a more open canyon with no pronounced vertical walls. Riparian habitat along the creek of willows and small cottonwoods, with some flooded meadows and marshy cattail areas, and scattered piñon pine on hillsides. www.wildlife.state.co.us

Viewing information: Primitive roads follow riparian corridors up both creeks. Watch for raptors along the cliffs above La Jara Creek, including great horned owls, golden and bald eagles, and red-tailed, rough-legged, and Swainson's hawks. Birds to watch for include goldfinches, robins, Swainson's thrushes, Clark's nutcrackers, pinyon jays, flickers, orioles, magpies, cliff swallows, spotted towhees, song sparrows, violet-green and tree swallows. Good winter range for deer and elk. Watch for them on sunny slopes in cold weather, and among riparian habitat. Mammals include thirteen-lined and Wyoming ground squirrels, pine squirrels, marmots, coyotes, cottontails, mountain lions. Look for bighorn sheep at the top of the canyon. Hot springs keep the waters of Hot Creek at 54 degrees, attracting a variety of aquatic wildlife. CDOW uses these warm waters as a native nursery for the Rio Grande sucker and Rio Grande chub reintroduction programs. Waterfowl and shorebirds are more abundant along Hot Creek, including mergansers, mallards, shovelers, gadwalls, cinnamon and green-winged teal. Raptors include those of La Jara Creek plus prairie falcons, sharp-shinned hawks, and harriers. The stream also hosts frogs and garter snakes. Muskrats, beavers, coyotes, bobcats, mountain lions, deer, elk, and an occasional pronghorn and bighorn sheep at this site. Both areas are closed from December 1 to April 30 to vehicle use, but can be accessed on foot.

Ownership: CDOW (719-587-6900)

Size: 6,854 acres

Closest town: Monte Vista, 20 miles; lodging, restaurants

Directions: See map this page

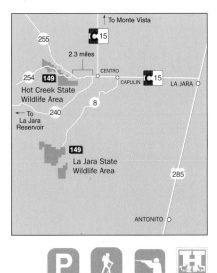

ROCKY MOUNTAINS

155

Description: This auto tour begins along Forest Road 250 east of Terrace Reservoir in open grasslands and piñon-juniper woodlands, then travels through riparian habitat of narrow-leaf cottonwood and willow along the Alamosa River, across Stunner Pass and down the Conejos River Canyon to Antonito. Higher elevations are mixed forest of Douglas-fir and white fir. A patch of lodgepole pine was planted to revegetate borrow pits on Stunner Pass—this is the southern extreme of its range. Engelmann spruce and subalpine fir on top of Stunner Pass, dropping down into willows in Conejos River Canyon. **Be aware that the Alamosa River is a Superfund site** due to mining pollution. **www.fs.fed.us**

Viewing information: Before you get to the canyon, watch in open areas for pronghorn. Many deer inhabit the piñon-juniper habitat. Elk use the area in winter. Due to pollution, there are no fish in the river, but watch for warblers, flycatchers, woodpeckers, jays, and various other birds in the riparian habitat along the river. Mountain lions and bears are occasionally seen. Watch for bighorn sheep above Terrace Reservoir on the north cliffs and in the Conejos River Canyon at a narrows called The Pinnacles. Look here also for moose.

Ownership: USFS (719-274-8971), PVT

Size: 75-mile drive

Closest town: Monte Vista, 15 miles; lodging, restaurants

Directions: *See map this page*

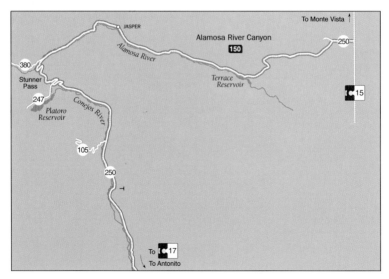

Description: An outstanding 75-mile scenic drive from South Fork to Lake City, via Creede. Route passes through mountain meadows, riverine mountain riparian areas along the Rio Grande River, and high-elevation forest of spruce/fir and aspen. Crossing the Continental Divide at Spring Creek Pass, the route winds over Slumgullion Pass into Lake City. Outstanding vistas, with good views of alpine regions, cascading waterfalls, geological formations, and historic and cultural sites. www.coloradobyways.org

Viewing information: Moose were released between the Hinsdale County line and north to Spring Creek Pass in 1991 and 1992; watch for them in willow bottoms. In winter look for elk at dawn and dusk at the Coller State Wildlife Area. Deer might be seen anywhere year-round. Bighorn sheep are often visible from the highway on cliffs and south-facing slopes, especially fall and winter. Best spots are Blue Creek to Wagon Wheel Gap and Seepage Creek to Clear Creek. Bald eagles are seen along the Rio Grande in winter. In summer watch for golden eagles, goshawks, red-tailed hawks, ravens, coyotes, and marmots. High-elevation forests offer good summertime songbird viewing. The Silver Thread Interpretive Center in South Fork has maps and information on the area.

Ownership: USFS (Silver Thread Interpretive Center, 719-873-5512), CDOW, PVT, BLM

Size: 75 miles

Closest town: South Fork; Creede; Lake City; restaurants, lodging

Directions: See map this page

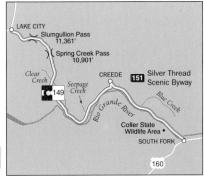

ROCKY MOUNTAINS

Moose were reintroduced to Colorado in the late 1970s, and their range is expanding. Wet areas dominated by willows and adjacent to coniferous forests make ideal moose habitat.
DENNIS HENRY

157

Description: This auto tour begins just south of Creede, traveling north through town and into the historic mining district in Willow Creek Canyon, with its dramatic remnants from Creede's mining days. Narrow, steep, rocky canyon with swift-flowing streams, high-elevation spruce-fir forest, and open meadows in the upper part of Windy Gulch.

Viewing information: Best time to combine the historic tour with wildlife viewing is in evenings from mid-May through October. Tour brochure, available at site number one about a half mile north of town, is the best route guide. Between the Commodore and Midwest Mines (tour sites two and seven), watch for beavers, their dams, ponds, and lodges along West Willow Creek. Moose visit these ponds and surrounding willows. Search the steep, rocky slopes on the west side for bristlecone pines. Watch for soaring golden eagles. Site 10, the Equity Mine, is a good place for marmots, golden-mantled ground squirrels, chipmunks, and more beavers and moose. Watch for elk around the edges of the high parks in this area. Check high-elevation forest for Steller's jays, chickadees, juncos, woodpeckers, and other nesting birds, as well as pine squirrels. Between sites 13 and 14, watch for marmots and pikas. The meadow beyond is very good for deer, elk, coyotes, and grassland birds.

Ownership: PVT (Creede Chamber of Commerce, 719-658-2374), USFS

Size: 17 miles

Closest town: Creede, in town; lodging, restaurants

Directions: See map this page

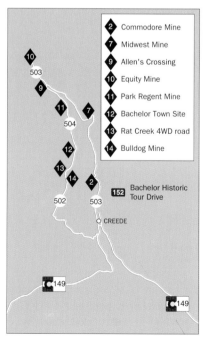

Description: High-altitude reservoirs at 10,000 feet in elevation with extensive willow community and sedge wetlands, surrounded by high-elevation forest of spruce and fir on north-facing slopes and grasslands with aspen groves on south-facing slopes. Bottom of glaciated valley is fairly flat and wide. The stream winds down through wet meadows of grasses, sedges, and willows. www.wildlife.state.co. us

Viewing information: The wetlands at the upper ends of each lake provide nesting habitat for waterfowl and water birds, and the lakes attract migrating birds. In summer look for lesser scaup, green-winged teal, common mergansers, wigeons, gadwalls, ruddy ducks, mallards, geese, coots, eared grebes, black-crowned night herons on the lakes and associated wetlands. Check below the lakes for beavers and their dams and lodges along South Clear Creek. Between the spillway and Colorado Highway 149, scan the willows for moose.

Check open areas for elk, prairie dogs, marmots. A great variety of songbirds inhabit surrounding forests in summer. Watch also for bald eagles around the lakes. On summer mornings and evenings listen for snipe winnowing over wet meadows.

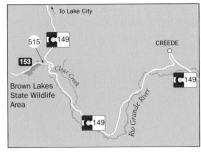

Ownership: CDOW (719-587-6900)

Size: 160 acres

Closest town: Creede, 25 miles; lodging, restaurants

Directions: See map this page

This scenic view of Brown Lakes State Wildlife Area from Colorado 149 offers a mosaic of meadows, forests, ponds, and high mountains. DANIEL LARSON

ROCKY MOUNTAINS

Description: This four-wheel-drive back country byway, much of it above timberline, offers good viewing of high-alpine tundra and spectacular scenery of the rugged San Juan Mountains. From Lake City the route goes up the Lake Fork of the Gunnison River and over Cinnamon Pass. It passes the ghost town of Animas Forks with numerous old buildings still standing. Cresting Engineer Pass, the route follows Henson Creek back to Lake City. The loop, also accessible from Silverton and Ouray, traverses a variety of high country habitats—alpine zone above timberline, high-elevation forests, open mountain meadows, and high-mountain riparian zones along streams and wetlands. Several roadside pullouts have historical markers. Route is open late May or early June through late October. www.co.blm.gov

Viewing information: Watch for alpine dwellers such as ptarmigan, marmots, and pikas. Elk and deer may also be visible. High-elevation forests are home to dusky grouse, chickarees, gray jays, Clark's nutcrackers, goshawks, and numerous other birds that find abundant food here in late summer. Watch for beaver dams along the Lake Fork of the Gunnison River and Henson Creek, and waterfowl on Lake San Cristobal. In late July and early August alpine wildflowers bloom in brilliant purples, yellows, reds, and blues.

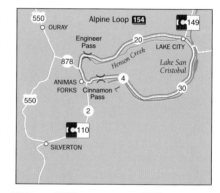

Ownership: BLM (970-641-0471)

Size: 45-mile loop drive

Closest town: Lake City; Silverton; Ouray; restaurants, lodging

Directions: See map this page

Visitors to the Alpine Loop Back Country Byway can hike to Sloan Lake on 14,048-foot Handies Peak. The trail leads 1.5 miles along Grizzly Gulch in the Handies Peak Wilderness Study Area.

JACK OLSON

Description: Open mountain grasslands along Forest Road 631, with riparian habitat of narrowleaf cottonwood, willow, and blue spruce along Williams Creek and mixed ponderosa pine-oakbrush on uplands. Wet meadows and high-elevation wetlands of sedges, rushes, marsh marigolds, willow, with cottonwoods and aspen in drier areas, surround the reservoir. Extensive willow complex above the reservoir. From Williams Creek Reservoir, trailheads lead into the Weminuche Wilderness. **www.fs.fed.us**

Viewing information: Gunnison's prairie dogs, ground squirrels, and mice in open country along the FR 631 leading to the reservoir attract a variety of hunting raptors. Rough-legged and ferruginous hawks in fall and winter; redtailed hawks year-round, kestrels common in spring and summer. Goshawks, sharp-shinned and Cooper's hawks in wooded uplands. Bald eagles are often seen in the area in winter. The reservoir hosts a large variety of waterfowl in spring and summer including goldeneyes, lesser scaup, pintails, gadwalls, bluewinged and cinnamon teal. Songbirds include tanagers; violet-green swallows; warbling vireos; yellow, Wilson's and McGillivray's warblers; white-crowned, song, fox, and chipping sparrows; various flycatchers. Moose are occasionally seen feeding in wet meadows and bighorn sheep can be spotted in winter on the cliffs above the reservoir. Maps and recreation information available at the Pagosa Ranger District office in Pagosa Springs.

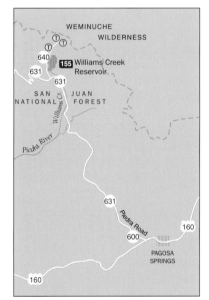

Ownership: USFS (970-264-2268)

Size: 1,200 acres

Closest town: Pagosa Springs, 13 miles; lodging, restaurants

Directions: See map this page

The northern leopard frog inhabits beaver ponds, streams, and marshes in Colorado up to elevations of about 11,000 feet.
DAVID F. TONEY

ROCKY MOUNTAINS

161

Description: A spectacular 105-foot-high waterfall along Fall Creek, which drains the southwest side of the Treasure Mountains. Good view down the wide San Juan River valley. Mature cottonwoodlands along the river with adjacent grassy mountain meadows. Surrounding mountain slopes rocky and steep with aspen and coniferous forests of ponderosa pine, Douglas-fir and white fir at lower elevations, and subalpine fir and Engelmann spruce higher up. Surrounding peaks range up to nearly 13,000 feet with alpine habitat on higher peaks, accessible from the top of Wolf Creek Pass. www.fs.fed.us

Viewing information: One of few sites to see black swifts in Colorado. These colonial birds nest behind the waterfall and in niches in rocky cliffs adjacent to the waterfall. Best viewing is early morning and late afternoon until dark, from late July through early September. At dusk watch for them bathing in the creek at the brink of the falls where the water falls over the cliff edge. You may see them fly directly through the falling water. Also watch the rushing stream for American dippers flying along the creek or jumping into the water. White-throated swifts nest in surrounding cliffs and hunt the air space above. Watch also for violet-green swallows, Williamson's and red-naped sapsuckers, western tanagers, pine siskins, mountain chickadees, brown creepers, gray jays, ruby-crowned kinglets, warbling vireos, hermit thrushes, yellow-rumped warblers, dark-eyed juncos. Check open meadows for elk and deer. Chipmunks and golden-mantled ground squirrels are abundant. A quarter-mile-long graded trail begins at the restrooms and ends at the falls. Interpretive signs along the trail discuss native wildlife, forest ecology, and geology of the San Juan Mountains. Elevated footbridge across the stream gorge and viewing platform at the base of the waterfall.

Ownership: USFS (970-264-2268)

Size: 100 acres

Closest town: Pagosa Springs, 15 miles; lodging, restaurants

Directions: *See map this page*

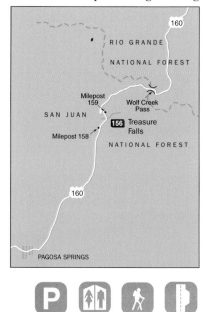

Description: Located within Navajo State Park, just south of the bridge over the Piedra River along Colorado Highway 151, the Navajo Overlook lies in a scenic setting overlooking the river, on the old railroad bed of the historic Denver and Rio Grande narrow gauge rail line. The shelter is next to a railroad bridge about 30 feet above the river. View of the river and the Southern Ute Indian Reservation. Cottonwood riparian habitat along the river with piñon-juniper and oakbrush on drier hillsides. www.parks.state.co.us

Viewing information: Mule deer, foxes, elk, wild turkeys year-round. Black bears and mountain lions sometimes seen. River otters have been spotted along the Piedra River both up and downstream from the overlook. Variety of birds common, including bluebirds, six species of swallows, cedar waxwings, dippers, black-chinned hummingbirds, Lewis's woodpeckers, white-faced ibis in migration. Watch for bald and golden eagles in winter, some bald eagles year-round. The Navajo State Park Visitor Center has interpretive exhibits and a bookstore. Further watchable wildlife opportunities within the main park and at Navajo Reservoir.

Ownership: State Parks (970-883-2208)

Size: 5 acres

Closest town: Arboles, 2 miles; lodging, restaurants

Directions: See map this page

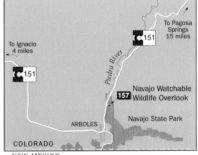

ROCKY MOUNTAINS

Description: A designated Archaeological Area and National Historic Site with ruins of the Chacoan Ancestral Pueblo culture. From the parking lot, a steep, one-mile trail leads to Chimney Rock, located atop a mesa. Visitors must stay on trails. Piñon-juniper and oakbrush with some ponderosa pine and Douglas-fir, intermixed with grassy meadows. Good scenic vistas of the Piedra Valley and Chimney Rock Pinnacles. A fire tower atop the mesa is open to the public. **You must have a permit or be on a guided tour to enter the area.** Volunteers and Forest Service staff conduct daily guided tours and operate the Visitor Center Cabin, open daily May 15 to September 30 from 9 a.m. to 4:30 p.m. www.chimneyrockco.org

Viewing information: Good chance of seeing deer, elk, and other mammals. Short-horned and fence lizards and rattlesnakes in sunny, rocky areas. Wild turkeys, dusky grouse, prairie falcons, ravens, crows, and swifts often visible at the site. Many golden and bald eagles may be seen in the valley. Tarantulas visible during fall migration. During the nesting season (March through September), access to a lookout tower to view the peregrine falcon aerie is by guided tour only. The half mile surrounding the nest is seasonally closed to any human activity. Rattlesnake sightings frequent.

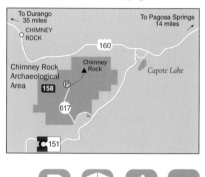

Ownership: USFS (970-883-5359 in season, 970-264-2287 off-season)

Size: 3,160 acres

Closest town: Pagosa Springs, 21.5 miles; restaurants, lodging

Directions: *See map this page*

Short-horned lizards have short spines for protection from predators. The lizards are partial to lowland habitats, where their natural coloring matches the local soil and provides additional protection. LAUREN J. LIVO AND STEVE WILCOX

Description: Trail winds through mixed forest with views of the Animas River valley. Interpretive stops explain the geology, forest ecology, wildlife, and human history of the site. www.fs.fed.us

Viewing information: Watch for eagles, turkey vultures, and several hawk species. Numerous songbirds. Jays, woodpeckers, red-naped sapsuckers, hummingbirds, ravens, and magpies are also found. Good place for chipmunks, ground squirrels, gray-phase Abert's squirrels, porcupines, and coyotes. Also elk, mule deer, and black bear. Reptiles include horned lizards, skinks, and various snakes.

Ownership: USFS (970-884-1400)

Size: 0.7 mile

Closest town: Durango, 9.5 miles; restaurants, lodging

Directions: *See map this page*

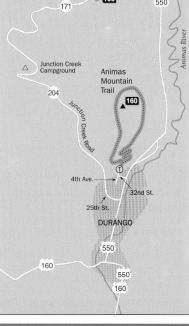

Description: This is a rest stop for migrating birds. A trail loops six miles from the city limit around the top of this 8,400-foot mountain. www.co.blm.gov

Viewing information: Peregrine falcons can be observed hunting swallows on the cliffs. Winter roost site for bald eagles. Watch for golden eagles, red-tailed and ferruginous hawks, and turkey vultures. Lots of ravens and jays. Concentrations of songbirds, on south-facing slopes. Winter range for deer and elk. Watch for chipmunks, ground squirrels, and gray-phase Abert's squirrels.

Ownership: BLM (970-247-4874)

Size: 2,700 acres

Closest town: Durango; restaurants, lodging

Directions: *See map above*

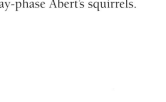

ROCKY MOUNTAINS

Description: This state fish hatchery offers a museum and visitor center with mounted displays and videos and some interpretive exhibits. Visitor center (970-375-6766) is open Tuesday through Saturday, May 1 to September 3 from 10 A.M. to 4 P.M. Visitors may feed the fish in the raceways. Raceways open for viewing 8 a.m. to 4 p.m. daily. Interpretive displays are along a 0.25-mile nature trail on the edge of the property. **www.wildlife.state.co us**

Viewing information: Eggs from rainbow, brook, brown, and cutthroat trout are hatched and raised here, then released into the wild to stock lakes and streams. Pools contain fingerlings (fish two to four inches long) and catchables (eight to twelve inches long).

Ownership: CDOW (970-247-0855)

Size: Five acres

Closest town: Durango, in town; restaurants, lodging

Directions: *See map this page*

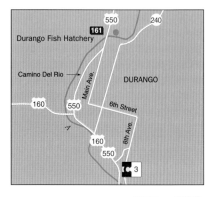

Located downtown on the Animas River, the Durango Fish Hatchery offers visitors the chance to view trout culture practices that are key to maintaining the quality of Colorado fisheries. GEOFF TISCHBIEN

Description: A driving tour along a spectacular scenic byway through the San Juan Mountains of southern Colorado, traveling across some of Colorado's most spectacular mountain passes. The route passes through diverse habitats, including agricultural areas, oakbrush, willow riparian, aspen forests, spruce-fir forest, mountain meadows, wet high-elevation meadows, rocky mountain slopes, alpine tundra. Outstanding scenic views. **www.coloradobyways.org**

Viewing information: Fall through spring elk are abundant. Watch for them in open areas and along the Animas River, a good place also for bald eagles in winter. Canada geese resident along the river. Foxes are sometimes seen and occasionally black bears in the warm months. Summer excellent for birding. Nearly 60 percent of Colorado's breeding bird species can be seen in the diverse habitats along the route. Golden eagles, goshawks, and red-tailed hawks can be seen in summer soaring overhead. At lakes along the highway you may see osprey in flight or perched in trees. Watch also for mountain bluebirds and kestrels. Boreal owls numerous in spruce-fir forests, though rarely seen. Maps and information available at San Juan National Forest supervisor's office in Durango and at Mancos-Dolores ranger district office in Dolores. Forest Service and BLM visitor centers in Silverton, Mancos, Dolores, and Durango offer checklists and other information in the summer months.

Ownership: USFS (970-884-2512), PVT, county

Size: 236-mile loop

Closest town: Durango, Silverton, Telluride, Dolores, Cortez; lodging, restaurants

Directions: See map this page

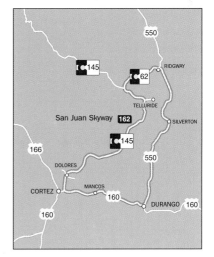

A meadow of blooming mule's ear provides a stunning foreground to the San Juan Mountains.
SHERM SPOELSTRA

ROCKY MOUNTAINS

Description: Located atop the slopes of Telluride Ski Area at 10,500 feet, the trails pass through high-elevation forest of Engelmann spruce and subalpine fir on the upper portions of the trail and aspen on the lower half. There are several very large, old-growth Douglas-firs along the trail. The Naturewatch Loop leaves from the St. Sophia Gondola Station, looping three-tenths of a mile through wooded terrain with dramatic views of the Telluride/San Miguel River valley and surrounding San Juan Mountains. Hiking and mountain biking trails pass down the mountain slope for 2 miles, often through deep forest, to Mountain Village.

Viewing information: Mule deer are often seen in the area of the ridge trail. Watch for elk across the valley on south-facing slopes of the Sneffels Range. Abert's squirrels are abundant. Watch also for chipmunks, pikas, and marmots near the old rock quarry about halfway down the trail. Birds include Steller's and gray jays, magpies, ravens, dusky grouse, red-tailed hawks, golden eagles. In wooded areas watch for sapsuckers, pine grosbeaks, kinglets, mountain chickadees, hermit thrushes, robins, and other songbirds that nest in high-altitude forests. Access the trails by riding the gondola to the St. Sophia Gondola Station (the ride is presently free), then hiking down. Snowshoe naturalist tours during ski season for a fee.

Ownership: Telluride Ski and Golf, USFS (970-327-4261)

Size: 2.3 miles of trails

Closest town: Telluride, 1 mile; lodging, restaurants

Directions: *See map this page*

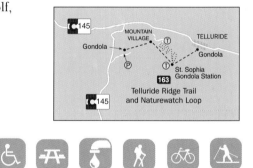

The white stripe above the eye helps distinguish the mountain chickadee from its cousin, the black-capped. Both nest in the mountains in summer, though mountain chickadees are generally found at higher altitudes, and move to lower elevations for winter.
MACK AND SHARON JOHNSON

Description: The Priest Lakes are located above 10,000 feet in spruce/fir and aspen forest interspersed with grassy meadows. Beaver ponds and willow/sedge riparian areas are found below the lakes along the Lake Fork of the San Miguel River. Nearby Matterhorn Campground is located in a high-elevation forest of Engelmann spruce and subalpine fir with patches of aspen. Trails lead into the Lizard Head Wilderness with good access to areas above timberline from nearby Lizard Head Pass. The site is located on the San Juan Skyway, Colorado Highway 145. Camping is primitive. **www.fs.fed.us**

Viewing information: Watch for dabbling ducks and grebes. You may see buffleheads and goldeneyes. Elk and deer are occasionally visible. Active beaver colonies along the creek. Watch for songbirds among the willows and in the high-elevation forest: warblers, nutcrackers, gray and Steller's jays, mountain chickadees, pine grosbeaks, red crossbills, and juncos. Forest raptors include Cooper's and sharp-shinned hawks. Also red-tailed hawks and golden eagles in open areas. Wetlands areas attract spotted sandpipers and killdeer.

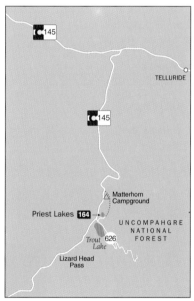

Ownership: USFS (970-327-4261)

Size: 30 acres

Closest town: Telluride, 10.25 miles; restaurants, lodging

Directions: *See map this page*

The pine grosbeak's heavy, crushing bill identifies it as a seed eater. Its two-note "chirrups" can often be heard by chairlift riders at Colorado ski resorts.
HARRY ENGELS

ROCKY MOUNTAINS

Description: A high-altitude reservoir surrounded by spruce/fir forest, with some aspen and meadowland. A small willow community wetland is found where Fall Creek feeds into the lake. Four major trail systems access the Lizard Head Wilderness from the area. A very scenic site, with a backdrop of Flattop, Middle, and Dolores Peaks, and the 14,000-foot summits of Mt. Wilson, Wilson Peak, and El Diente Peak to the southeast. The road from Beaver Park to Woods Lake is a scenic drive through high-elevation forest. **www.fs.fed.us**

Viewing information: Look for an active beaver colony in the marshy area along Fall Creek. Watch for ducks—mallards, teal, an occasional bufflehead or merganser—on the lake or in the wetlands. Killdeer, sandpipers, and various shorebirds may be seen around the water's edge. Numerous woodland and riparian birds found along waterways: downy and hairy woodpeckers, red-naped sapsuckers, gray jays, Clark's nutcrackers, red crossbills, flickers, mountain bluebirds, various warblers, hummingbirds, and dusky grouse. Woods Lake is a major elk-calving site, so there's a good chance to view elk in June.

Ownership: CDOW, USFS (970-327-4261)

Size: 60 acres

Closest town: Telluride, 21 miles; restaurants, lodging

Directions: *See map this page*

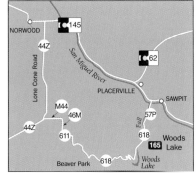

The green-winged teal's shiny green head patch makes it easily identifiable. A member of the duck family, the green-winged teal is half the size of the more common mallard.
CLAUDE STEELMAN

Colorado Plateau

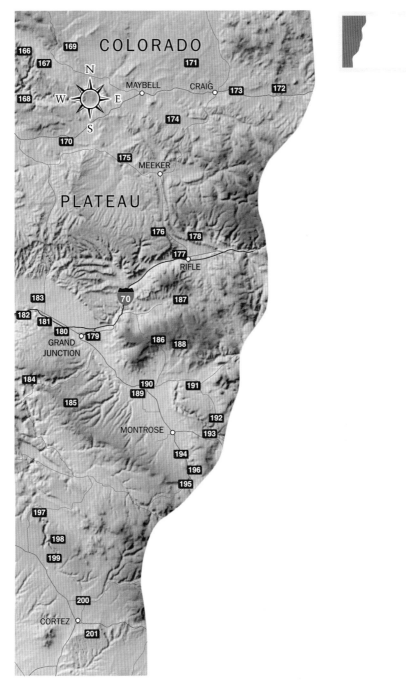

The Colorado Plateau dominates western Colorado, a land of dry shrublands of greasewood, big sagebrush, and rabbitbrush as well as piñon pine and juniper woodlands mixed with grassy meadows.

Rivers lined with cottonwoods and tamarisk wind through rocky canyons and mesas, and coniferous forests mark higher elevations.

Description: A series of ponds and wet meadows along the Green River managed for waterfowl and migratory songbirds, featuring steep rocky slopes, alluvial benches, and bottomlands along the river. Check at the visitor center for specific viewing opportunities. **www.fws.gov**

Viewing information: Prime area for viewing Canada geese, mallards, redheads, canvasbacks, green-winged and cinnamon teal, ruddy ducks, common mergansers, and other ducks. Other birds include coots, great blue herons, three grebe species, white-faced ibis, red-winged and yellow-headed blackbirds, Wilson's snipes, Wilson's phalaropes, several sandpipers, kingfishers, golden and bald eagles, shrikes, hummingbirds, swallows, and other songbirds. The bird checklist includes 220 species. Watch for mule deer, moose, coyotes, beavers, muskrats, and pronghorn. Watch for signs on Colorado Highway 318 marking the east and west ends of the refuge.

Ownership: USFWS (970-365-3613)

Size: 13,455 acres

Closest town: Maybell, 63 miles; restaurants, lodging

Directions: *See map below*

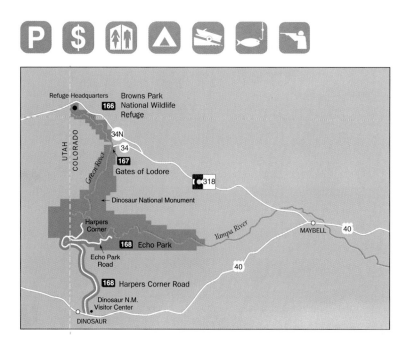

167. GATES OF LODORE

Description: Within the northern portion of Dinosaur National Monument stands the striking portal into the Canyon of Lodore on the Green River. Box elder/cottonwood riparian habitat along the river, canyon walls and benches typified by sagebrush, and piñon-juniper woodlands with Douglas-fir in moist areas. A 1-mile nature trail begins at the campground. Check at the visitor center for information on the site and boating permits. **www.nps.gov**

Viewing information: Lots of migrant waterfowl, including scaup, mallards, pintails, and wigeons. Good chance to see raptors, including golden eagles at the campground, occasional falcons as well as hawks in the canyon. Watch for gnatcatchers, kingbirds, flycatchers, warblers, and other songbirds. Side-blotched and eastern fence lizards are common in rocky areas. River otters on river. Beaver in the Browns Park area, particularly in evening. Boating trips allow viewing of bighorn sheep.

Ownership: NPS (970-374-3000)

Size: 60 acres   **Closest town:** Maybell, 63 miles; restaurants, lodging

Directions: See map opposite page

168. HARPERS CORNER ROAD/ECHO PARK

Description: A self-guided tour from the Dinosaur National Monument visitor center to Echo Park. Echo Park is a sandy beach area at the junction of the Yampa and Green Rivers beneath magnificent sandstone cliffs. Drier slopes and benches typified by sagebrush and piñon-juniper woodlands, with Douglas-fir on north exposures along the canyon rim and box elder/willow communities along the river. Check first at the visitor center for information and road conditions into Echo Park. **Boating permit required. www.nps.gov**

Viewing information: Mule deer are usually visible from the road; occasional elk and bighorn sheep. Waterfowl, some shorebirds, and possibly river otter or beaver are seen along the rivers; songbirds in riparian zones. Good raptor watching, with eagles, hawks, kestrels, and prairie falcons common. Watch for peregrine falcons around cliff areas in Echo Park. **Cliffs are closed to climbing in spring and summer due to nesting.** Watch cliff overhangs for swallows, and canyon and rock wrens.

Ownership: NPS (970-374-3000)   **Size:** 41-mile drive, one way

Closest town: Dinosaur, 61 miles; restaurants, lodging

Directions: See map opposite page

Description: A large, arid basin typified by sagebrush and salt desert shrubs, ringed by juniper-covered hills. The basin rim is characterized by rocky sandstone outcrops. A series of drainages runs through the basin, but they are dry most of the year. Vermillion Bluffs on the northwest edge of the rim is a badlands-like area. The arid basin offers dramatic, scenic terrain. **County roads are passable by passenger car only in dry weather.** www.co.blm.gov

Viewing information: The large, sagebrush basin is good winter range for pronghorn. Golden eagles are often seen hunting over the basin; they roost and nest along the rim. Burrowing owls inhabit prairie dog towns April through August. Great horned owls are common. With few trees in the area, they roost in cavities in the banks of washes and drainages. Other raptors include ferruginous and red-tailed hawks and prairie falcons.

Ownership: BLM (970-826-5000)

Size: 100,000 acres

Closest town: Maybell, 75 miles; restaurants, lodging

Directions: *See map this page*

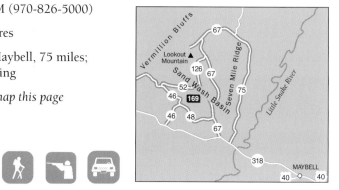

Fleet-footed pronghorn have been clocked at eighty miles per hour. Their speed and keen eyesight help them avoid danger in their sagebrush and dry grassland plains habitat.
DENNIS HENRY

Description: Shallow reservoir set within semi-desert shrublands. Surrounding lands form a series of low ridges and broad valleys cut by deeply eroded drainage channels. Uplands are typically Gardner and mat saltbush, with black greasewood and big sagebrush in valleys and channels. Dense wetland vegetation of cattails, bulrushes, sedges, and rushes surrounds the reservoir, with some cottonwoods, box elders, tamarisk, and Russian olive, giving it the feel of an oasis amid the high desert. **www.co.blm.gov**

Viewing information: Some pronghorn seen year-round. Large concentrations of elk in the low hills to the south and along major Wolf Creek drainages in January and February. Excellent waterfowl viewing on the reservoir, particularly during migration. Look for mallards, pintails, shovelers, gadwalls, blue- and green-winged teal, buffleheads, common goldeneyes, ring-necked duck, and lesser scaup. Occasional redhead or canvasback. Nesting ruddy ducks, pied-billed grebes, and coots. Virginia rails, soras, and yellow-headed blackbirds nest in bulrushes. White-faced ibis are regular migrants, as well as avocets, willets, yellowlegs, dowitchers, phalaropes, Franklin's and ring-billed gulls, and eared grebes. Watch also for snowy egrets, black terns, black-crowned night herons. Abundant nesting sage and Brewer's sparrows, sage thrashers. Active white-tailed prairie dog colonies attract burrowing owls and ferruginous hawks (nesting in the area). Loggerhead shrikes and mockingbirds nest along the channels of Wolf Creek, 1.5 miles east. **Road is impassable winter and early spring.** Call BLM for current conditions.

Ownership: BLM (970-878-3800)

Size: 20 acres

Closest town: Dinosaur, 23 miles; lodging, restaurants

Directions: *See map this page*

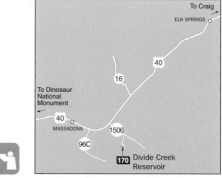

The Virginia rail is a shy marsh bird that feeds among the cattails and emergent plants. Watch for them wading or standing in shallow water at the margin of aquatic vegetation and open water.
WENDY SHATTIL/BOB ROZINSKI

COLORADO PLATEAU

177

Description: A mountain shrub community of sagebrush, serviceberry, and snowberry with scattered piñon-juniper woodlands. A cliff area offers nesting habitat for raptors. There is a 3.5-mile interpretive trail. **www.co.blm.gov**

Viewing information: Golden eagles can be observed soaring and hunting. **Keep away from the cliff face early March through early July when the birds are nesting.** Watch for turkey vultures soaring on the thermals. Small mammals you may see include white-tailed jackrabbits, cottontails, and Wyoming ground squirrels. Excellent viewing of shrubland songbirds, with lots of towhees, flycatchers, warblers, and pinyon jays. Mule deer use the area, and elk are seen during spring and fall migration. Pronghorn are sometimes visible on the drive to the mountain. Watch for bald eagles year-round along the Yampa River near Craig.

Ownership: BLM (970-826-5000)

Size: 800 acres

Closest town: Craig, 7.5 miles; restaurants, lodging

Directions: *See map this page*

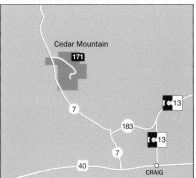

The magnificent golden eagle is one of the West's largest birds of prey. Mature golden eagles are distinguished by golden feathers on the nape of the head and neck.
W. PERRY CONWAY

Description: The Bottoms is flat to rolling country of grazing land and grain fields, with cottonwood riparian habitat along the Yampa River. Foothills terrain surrounds the valley bottom. Noncultivated land is typified by sagebrush, chokecherry, and serviceberry. Land is private so viewing is from the road.

Viewing information: Morgan Bottoms is a spring and fall staging area for migrating sandhill cranes. Watch for them flying overhead or feeding during the day in grain fields; in spring the cranes can be seen dancing and jumping. Largest concentrations occur in fall, when as many as 1,000 cranes gather. For information on spring viewing of sage, dusky, and sharp-tailed grouse, contact the Craig Chamber of Commerce and Sportsmen's Information Center (970-824-3046) for the Yampa Valley Grouse Brochure and information on locations of grouse leks.

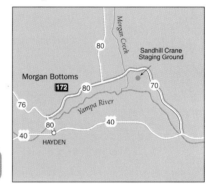

Ownership: PVT

Size: 10-mile drive

Closest town: Hayden; restaurants, lodging

Directions: *See map this page*

The male sandhill crane begins his courtship ritual with a leap into the air. The spring dance in open fields occurs prior to the cranes' relocation to nesting areas elsewhere.
WENDY SHATTIL/
BOB ROZINSKI

COLORADO PLATEAU

Description: Six sites along the Yampa River between Hayden and Dinosaur National Monument are accessible by auto or by river float trip. At **Park Headquarters** is a 70-acre mix of meadows and cottonwoodlands along a quarter mile of the Yampa River. The **Yampa River State Wildlife Area** (Habitat Stamp required) is an 863-acre parcel of narrowleaf cottonwood riparian habitat, wet meadows, and a large wetlands. **Elkhead Reservoir** has riparian habitat above and below the reservoir, surrounded by flat agricultural land and grasslands, with some hills and bluffs. **Duffy River Access** offers riparian habitat along the river with sagebrush uplands surrounded by rolling hills and agricultural land. **Maybell Bridge** is a mix of riparian and sagebrush shrublands habitat along the Yampa River. **East Cross Mountain** offers a diverse mix of piñon-juniper woodlands, sagebrush grassland, cliffs, bluffs, rolling hills, riparian woodlands, and agricultural fields along the river bottom. www.wildlife.state.co.us www.parks.state.co.us www.nps.gov

Viewing information: Various waterfowl along the river and at Elkhead Reservoir, most abundant in fall—pintails, mallards, buffleheads, goldeneyes, ruddy ducks, Canada and snow geese. Wading and shorebirds in wetlands and along the riverbank include herons, stilts, killdeer, various sandpipers, and an occasional avocet. Sandhill cranes nest in the area and are seen in spring and early summer; **respect the cranes' nests and view from a distance**. Mule deer common along the edge of meadows; elk feed in wheat fields in winter. Best pronghorn viewing in fall and winter. An isolated herd of bighorn sheep inhabits East Cross Mountain. Coyotes, foxes, raccoons, badgers, muskrats, and beavers visible year-round, with occasional minks and long-tailed weasels along the river. Sage grouse inhabit shrublands with big sagebrush. East Cross Mountain is a good spot to find wintering flocks of sage grouse. Riparian birds include various warblers, sparrows, wrens, magpies, waxwings, tanagers,

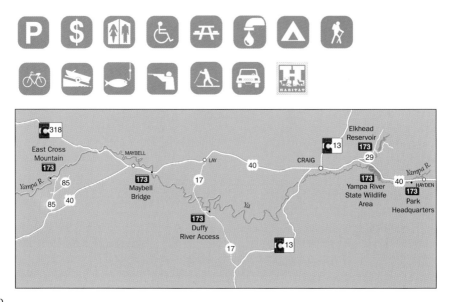

finches, crows, and flickers. Golden and bald eagles are best seen in winter. Hawks include red-tailed (year-round), Swainson's (summer), and rough-legged (winter). Turkey vultures common spring through fall. Jackrabbits, cottontails, ground squirrels, and chipmunks are plentiful. Western rattlesnakes are common in warm weather. Elk use East Cross Mountain in winter, and deer are abundant year-round. The visitor center at Park Headquarters will offer interpretive information. A highway pulloff overlook with interpretive panels at the state wildlife area is under construction. Other interpretive information at sites along U.S. Highway 40.

Ownership: CDOW; State Parks (970-276-2061)   **Size:** 70 miles

Closest town: Hayden, Craig; Maybell; lodging, restaurants

Directions: *See map opposite page*

Black-necked stilts are only one of many shore and wading birds that nest in the ponds and marshes of western Colorado. They are sometimes nicknamed "lawyer birds" for their black-and-white plumage and shrill, persistent calling.
SHERM SPOELSTRA

Description: A series of rolling, sagebrush-covered ridges and drainages provides important winter range for deer and elk and year-long habitat for pronghorn. **Check road conditions prior to winter visits.** A 70-mile loop can be made from Craig with excellent viewing of big game animals along County Road 17 in Axial Basin. www.co.blm.gov

Viewing information: Elk, mule deer, and pronghorn easily visible from the road. Watch for bald eagles where the highway crosses the Yampa River. Golden eagles and rough-legged hawks also winter in the basin. Keep an eye out for sage grouse. Small mammals include jackrabbits and cottontails, and occasional weasels and coyotes. Watch for winter grassland birds such as horned larks. Best viewing December to March.

Ownership: BLM (970-826-5000)

Size: 20-mile drive

Closest town: Craig, 27.5 miles; restaurants, lodging

Directions: See map this page

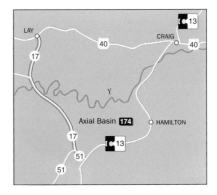

The cottontail—an adaptable, abundant, and often-seen Colorado resident—is found in brushy foothills terrain.
CLAUDE STEELMAN

Artificial nest boxes have helped increase declining populations of both western and mountain bluebirds across Colorado.

Western bluebirds may rear up to three broods of young in a season. The first brood often contains five hatchlings, with fewer in successive broods.
MARY TAYLOR YOUNG

Description: Upland areas around the reservoir are greasewood shrubland and grassland. Willow/hawthorn bottoms along the river, with a small, mixed stand of cottonwood and juniper. Wet meadows of cattail and bulrush, with tamarisk and saltgrass around old river oxbows. **www.wildlife.state.co.us**

Viewing information: Rio Blanco is a stopover point for migrating waterfowl and shorebirds, especially in spring. Watch for marbled godwits; avocets; phalaropes; dowitchers; willets; yellowlegs; cattle egrets; and occasional snowy and American egrets; and gulls, terns, and grebes. There is a great blue heronry in the cottonwoods just off the southwest boundary; good viewing from the road along the canal. Keep an eye out for loons, ospreys, swans, cranes, white pelicans, and diving ducks in spring and fall. Wintering bald eagles and rough-legged hawks are common along the White River. Many marsh and riparian songbirds in willow bottoms, and beaver are active along the river. Bring water as this site is remote.

Ownership: CDOW (970-878-6090), BLM (970-878-3601)

Size: 500 acres

Closest town: Meeker, 18 miles; restaurants, lodging

Directions: *See map below*

Great blue herons nest in heronries, colonies typically located in cottonwood groves. The large, long-legged anglers can commonly be seen near water.
W. PERRY CONWAY

Description: Rolling hills and rugged canyons offer a variety of habitats. Shrublands of oakbrush, sagebrush, and mountain-mahogany; willow riparian along several streams with some cottonwoods, grassy meadows, and wildflowers; spruce-fir and aspen forests in higher elevations. The Roan Cliffs offer majestic views of the Colorado River valley. **www.co.blm.gov**

Viewing information: Mornings and evenings in summer and fall offer good sightings of elk and mule deer. Black bears and mountain lions may be seen occasionally. Many small mammals such as porcupines, ground squirrels, jackrabbits, coyotes. Watch for golden eagles and prairie and peregrine falcons soaring and hunting along the Roan Cliffs. Other cliff-dwelling birds include white-throated swifts, violet-green and cliff swallows, rock wrens. Many nesting and migrant birds including nighthawks, Lewis's woodpeckers, ravens, magpies, mountain bluebirds, and a variety of flycatchers and vireos; broad-tailed, rufous and black-chinned hummingbirds; Steller's and scrub jays; Lucy's, yellow, yellow-rumped, and black-throated gray warblers.

Ownership: BLM (970-947-2800)

Size: 54,000 acres   **Closest town:** Rifle, 50 miles; lodging, restaurants

Directions: See map next page

If I look around I discover another world that lies directly at my feet.

Description: This shallow, 5-acre pond is surrounded by high-desert shrublands of sagebrush, saltbush, and greasewood. Pond itself not accessible but visitors can view wildlife from nearby benches. **www.fs.fed.us, www.co.blm.gov**

Viewing information: Good place for migrating waterfowl, including buffleheads, hooded mergansers, ruddy ducks, and shore and wading birds (phalaropes, snipes, western sandpipers). Nesting water birds include shovelers, pintails, blue-winged teal, coots, pied-billed grebes. Great blue herons common. Watch for bald eagles in winter. Belted kingfishers, six species of swallows, sage thrashers, blue grosbeaks, marsh wrens, mountain bluebirds, Bullock's orioles, black-chinned and broad-tailed hummingbirds, various flycatchers and warblers. Mule deer and beavers can be seen. Watch for bats on summer evenings. Maps, checklists, and publications available at the adjacent Rifle Ranger District office. Interpretive signs at the site.

Ownership: USFS (970-625-2371), BLM

Size: 25 acres

Closest town: Rifle, 1 mile; lodging, restaurants

Directions: *See map this page*

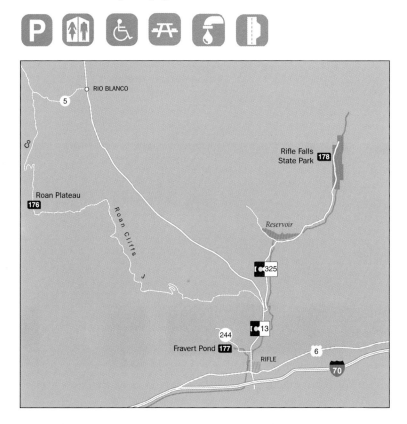

Description: A trio of 80-foot-high waterfalls and a series of limestone caves are the focal features of this park which lies within a steep-sided canyon. Abundant growth of box elder, hawthorn, chokecherry, and narrowleaf cottonwood along East Rifle Creek create a lush, grotto-like setting. Surrounding terrain of piñon pine-juniper woodlands, higher-elevation shrublands of oakbrush and mountain-mahogany, and pockets of spruce and fir. **www.parks.state.co.us**

Viewing information: Mammals include coyotes, mule deer, elk, skunks, raccoons, cottontails, chipmunks, ground squirrels. Best chance for spotting them is near the water at dawn and dusk. Mountain lions occasionally seen. With the diversity of habitats, many birds use the park, including black-headed grosbeaks, yellow and yellow-rumped warblers, lazuli buntings. Watch for dippers and kingfishers along the water. Of particular note are black swifts that nest behind the waterfall. Watch for them hunting insects above the falls. **Visitors should avoid the area behind the falls to protect the birds**, their nests, and their young. The park is important nesting habitat for harriers and golden eagles. Little brown bats use the caves in summer and may be seen hunting insects in the evening. **Be careful not to disturb these mammals if found roosting within the caves.**

Ownership: State Parks (970-625-1607)

Size: 92 acres

Closest town: Rifle, 14 miles; lodging, restaurants

Directions: *See map opposite page*

Three dramatic waterfalls and a series of limestone caves make Rifle Falls State Park a fascinating place to explore. SHERM SPOELSTRA

Description: Three wildlife viewing areas along the corridor of the Colorado River through the Grand Valley. Located at the confluence of the Colorado and Gunnison Rivers, **Grand Junction Wildlife Area** is a river-bottom park being restored with stands of native cottonwoods, shrublands, and grasslands and ponds designated for cultivation of endangered native Colorado River fishes. A riverfront trail traverses the **Colorado River Wildlife Area** through riparian habitat, passing near a large lake and backwater pools. A major restoration of wetlands is underway. A series of trails traverses the **Connected Lakes of Colorado River State Park**, reclaimed gravel pits along the river that are bordered by grasslands and riparian habitat of cottonwoods and box elder. www.parks.state.co.us

Viewing information: The lakes and backwaters of Colorado River Wildlife Area are very good for shorebirds, waterfowl, and raptors, especially during migration. Good birding in wooded and marshy areas, especially in the less-developed Grand Junction Wildlife Area. A parking lot, trail, and viewing blind overlooking a 5-acre pond are under development. Watch in uplands for mule deer, pheasants, and Gambel's quail, a southwestern species introduced into this part of Colorado. Beavers are present at all three sites. Note the beaver dams along the river backwater at Colorado River Wildlife Area, and in winter look here for large numbers of wintering Canada geese and dabbling ducks. There is a kiosk and paved trail around the lakes and along the river here. Watch for coyotes, cottontails, skunks, golden and bald eagles, osprey,

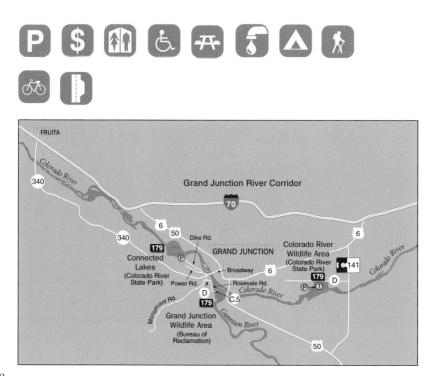

and a variety of hawks and owls. Portions of the wildlife areas are closed to protect wildlife but can be visited by school or environmental groups by prior arrangement with the Mesa County Land Conservancy. Connected Lakes and Colorado River Wildlife Area are tied to the Colorado River trail system.

Ownership: State Parks, BOR, Mesa County Land Conservancy

Size: 350 acres

Closest town: Grand Junction, 1 mile; lodging, restaurants

Directions: *See map opposite page*

Not native to Colorado, Gambel's quail was introduced into western Colorado as a game species beginning in the 1880s. Small populations of these southwestern birds are established around Grand Junction and Durango. SHERM SPOELSTRA

Description: An outstanding scenic area of red sandstone canyons and rock formations along the northern tip of the Uncompahgre Plateau overlooking the Grand Valley. Piñon-juniper forested mesas with some grassy areas, Gambel oak, sagebrush, and relic stands of Douglas-fir. Some cottonwoods, willows, and tamarisk grow along seasonal streams in the canyon bottoms. Inquire at the visitor center for specific viewing opportunities. **www.nps.gov**

Viewing information: Golden eagles and red-tailed hawks visible year-round, with turkey vultures April to September. Watch for bald eagles in winter along the Colorado River outside the monument. Active peregrine falcon aerie; watch for the adults hunting around cliffs. Scrub and pinyon jays, Gambel's quail, doves, magpies, canyon wrens, violet-green swallows, and white-throated swifts are all common. A variety of other songbirds may be seen. Mule deer are visible in winter around the visitor center, with occasional elk. Desert bighorn sheep inhabit Fruita Canyon and are visible from the roadside. Watch for tracks and sign of mountain lions. Good reptile viewing in sunny, rocky areas, with whiptails, bullsnakes, and collared, side-blotched, sagebrush, and eastern fence lizards all common. Camping fee required year-round. Nearby **Rattlesnake/Devil's Canyon** area on BLM land is home to 100 or more desert bighorn sheep, best observed from early March to late November. **Travel there requires a high-clearance vehicle.**

Ownership: NPS (970-858-3617), BLM

Size: 20,450 acres

Closest town: Grand Junction, 6 miles; Fruita, 3 miles; restaurants, lodging

Directions: See map this page

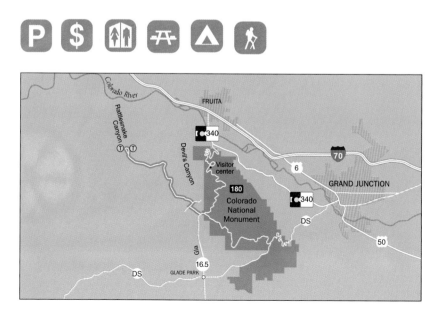

Description: This state wildlife area encompasses cottonwood riparian zones along the Colorado River. Horsethief is a transition zone of irrigated agricultural fields and wildlife feeding plots. The terrain rises into shrubby canyonlands of red sandstone rock formations and cliff faces, with scattered piñon-juniper woodlands. **www.wildlife.state.co.us**

Viewing information: Desert bighorn sheep are occasionally seen in rocky areas. Walk the Pollock Bench and Devil's Canyon trails into BLM land. Mule deer inhabit the area year-round, with greater concentrations in fall as they move into the fields to feed. Good waterfowl viewing along the river, especially in fall, including Canada geese, mallards and other dabbling ducks, and some wood ducks. Great blue herons use the area in summer; bald eagles are very visible along the river in winter. Watch also for golden eagles, peregrine falcons, and grassland raptors such as red-tailed and Swainson's hawks as well as quail and turkeys. A variety of songbirds uses the riparian habitat along the river in spring and summer. Waterfowl blinds along the river offer hidden viewing vantages. Two interpretive wildlife viewing loops pass near wetlands, riverside forests, ponds, and planted areas.

Ownership: CDOW (970-255-6100)

Size: 1,050 acres

Closest town: Fruita, 6.5 miles; restaurants, lodging

Directions: *See map this page*

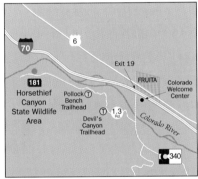

The collared lizard is easily recognized by its yellow and black neck collar. The reptile also is characterized by its pushup-like bobbing motion. This lizard basks on warm, rocky outcroppings in southern Colorado.
SHERM SPOELSTRA

COLORADO PLATEAU

191

Description: Semi-desert shrubland typified by greasewood along waterways, desert shrubs, Utah juniper on low mesas, and a sagebrush plain to the north. Grasses and flowering annual and perennial plants sweep across the valley floor. The Colorado River is to the south. Visitors traveling west along Interstate 70 first encounter the desert region of the Intermountain West at Rabbit Valley. **www.co.blm.gov**

Viewing information: Look for the dens of Ord's kangaroo rats in the sandy soil at the base of clumps of shrubs. At dawn and dusk and on moonlit nights watch for the 'roo rats bounding around in the pale light, possibly pursued by kit foxes. Listen and watch for rock wrens in rocky habitat. Other birds include Scott's orioles, gray vireos, gray flycatchers, pinyon jays, black-throated sparrows, sage sparrows, northern mockingbirds, and long-eared owls. Watch for bald and golden eagles, ferruginous, red-tailed, and rough-legged hawks and prairie falcons hunting over white-tailed prairie dog colonies, particularly in winter. Pronghorn seen north of the interstate. Reptiles to watch for include collared, leopard, side-blotched, and tree lizards. In late spring and early summer, visit the stands of juniper on the Utah border along M.80 Road west of Mack, for birds more typical of the Great Basin.

Ownership: BLM (970-244-3000)

Size: 15,748 acres

Closest town: Mack, 10 miles; restaurants

Directions: See map opposite page

If you venture out quietly on a moonlit night into the open shrublands of western Colorado, you may see Ord's kangaroo rats bounding around in the moonlight. Aptly named, these large-eyed rodents hop around on their hind legs like tiny kangaroos. CLAUDE STEELMAN

Description: The park includes two lakes—the large Highline Lake, a reservoir along Mack Wash, and the smaller Mack Mesa Lake—situated in high desert habitat surrounded by agricultural land, with the mesas and canyons of the Grand Valley beyond. The park is largely open-water habitat and open, grassy areas with some shade trees. **www.parks.state.co.us**

Viewing information: More than 150 species of birds recorded. The open water amid high desert attracts abundant waterfowl and shorebirds, with 5,000 to 10,000 birds sometimes seen in migration. Great blue herons, white pelicans, snowy egrets, avocets, stilts, willets, plovers, phalaropes, godwits, various sandpipers. Occasional loons and trumpeter and tundra swans. Raptors include both golden eagles and various hawks year-round, bald eagles in winter, and osprey in summer. Active prairie dog town and a very visible beaver lodge. Mule deer, coyotes, red foxes, cottontails. Watchable Wildlife kiosk and spotting scope on Highline Lake's east side, bird overlook with scope and interpretive panels on west side.

Ownership: State Parks (970-858-7208)

Size: 580 acres

Closest town: Fruita, 12 miles; lodging, restaurants

Directions: *See map this page*

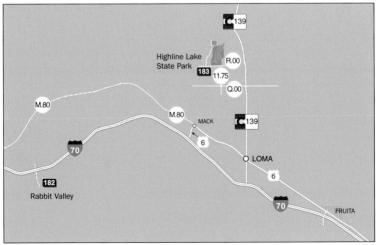

Description: This site lies along West Creek and up a south-facing slope within Unaweep Canyon. Part of the seep site is a BLM Area of Critical Environmental Concern, providing habitat for the rare Nokomis Fritillary butterfly. Riparian habitat, wet meadows and marsh surrounded by piñon-juniper woodlands. Springs and seeps on the hillside nurture a unique wild garden of relict plants rare or absent in the rest of the state. Poison ivy is abundant. **www.blm.gov**

Viewing information: Primary viewing is from a wide pullover 0.2 mile toward Gateway from the bridge at milepost 120 of Colorado Highway 141. **Use caution pulling off the road and leaving your vehicle.** The area on the far (north) side of West Creek is wet and mucky so stay on the south (highway) side of the creek for good wildlife viewing. Listen and watch for a rich array of songbirds May through July in riparian woodlands, including indigo bunting and, winter wren. June through late September excellent for butterflies, 67 species have been recorded. Watch for mule deer and elk along the highway for seven miles in both directions between December and April. No camping, motorized vehicles or wood-gathering is allowed in the natural area. Interpretive sign at site.

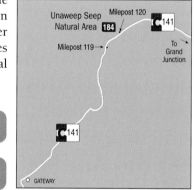

Ownership: BLM (303-244-3000)

Size: 80 acres

Closest town: Gateway, 7 miles

Directions: See map this page

Description: Mixed community of old-growth aspen and ponderosa pine. The trail passes through the forest to the rim of Carson Hole, where you can look into the canyon bottom to see willow riparian areas, wetlands, and beaver ponds along La Fair Creek. Trails lead along the rim and descend to the canyon floor through mixed conifer forest. **www.fs.fed.us**

Viewing information: Area of intense use by cavity nesting birds, offering a variety of species due to the age and diversity of the tree community. Nesting species include flammulated and pygmy owls, woodpeckers, sapsuckers, nuthatches, swallows, and western bluebirds. A variety of raptors use the area. Active beaver colony along the creek.

Ownership: USFS (970-242-8211) **Size:** 3-mile trail

Closest town: Grand Junction, 29 miles; restaurants, lodging

Directions: See map opposite page

Description: This national recreation trail follows the backbone of the Grand Mesa along a ridge rising 300 feet above the mesa plateau. Elevations along the trail range from 10,150 to 11,189 feet, the highest point on the mesa. This is a great geological site. Rocky cliffs drop off on both sides, with lakes visible at the bottom. Outstanding panoramic vistas of the entire mesa. Primarily high-elevation forest of spruce/fir and aspen, with open meadows. The trail is steep and rocky in places. Species checklist and brochure available at the visitor center at Cobbett Lake open daily in summer, weekends in winter. www.fs.fed.us

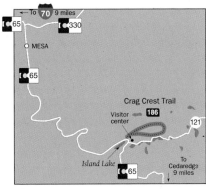

Viewing information: Golden eagles use the cliffs, and the rocky ridge is a raptor migration site. Good site to hear fall elk bugling. Lots of mule deer browse in meadows and around lake edges. Watch for pikas and marmots in rocky areas. Other mammals include chickarees, chipmunks, snowshoe hares, and porcupines. Many birds can be seen—ravens, woodpeckers, chickadees, hummingbirds, and dusky grouse.

Ownership: USFS (970-242-8211)

Size: 10-mile loop trail

Closest town: Cedaredge, 15 miles; restaurants, lodging

Directions: See map this page

Pikas spend the short summers gathering huge quantities of food and storing it away for the long winter. Their sharp whistle is a familiar sound in the Colorado high country. TOM TIETZ

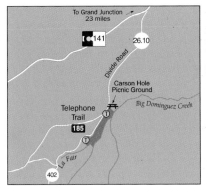

Description: A 900-acre reservoir surrounded by 900 acres of grasslands, rolling hills, and mountains on the north side of the Grand Mesa at an elevation of 8,000 feet. Mixed habitats of grassland, sagebrush, and shrublands with Gambel oak, rabbitbrush, sagebrush, chokecherry, serviceberry, snowberry, willow, and numerous wildflowers and grasses. Riparian woodlands and aspen forest. www.parks.state.co.us

Viewing information: Spring through fall are the best times for wildlife viewing. Small mammals include marmots, porcupines, weasels, rock squirrels, chipmunks, ground squirrels, skunks, and beavers. Elk, mule deer, coyotes, and red foxes can be seen year-round. Bald eagles and a variety of hawks hunt within the park. A variety of waterfowl, wading and shore birds, and songbirds can be seen, particularly during migration. Late September through mid-October watch and listen for migrating sandhill cranes, which feed and rest within the park. Visitor center offers interpretive exhibits and programs, and bookstore. Two-mile, self-guided nature trail. Ranger-led interpretive programs and nature walks on summer weekends and by request.

Ownership: State Parks (970-487-3407), BOR

Size: 1,800 acres

Closest town: Collbran, 12 miles; restaurant, lodging

Directions: *See map this page*

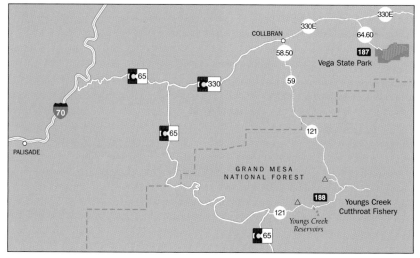

Description: A chain of five high-elevation reservoirs atop the Grand Mesa, surrounded by spruce-fir forest with stands of aspen. Habitats of the Grand Mesa, which rises from 6,000 to over 10,500 feet in elevation, include high-elevation forests, mountain meadows, mountain riparian, and shrublands. www.fs.fed.us

Viewing information: The reservoirs are managed for Colorado River cutthroat trout. Sunglasses with polarizing lenses enhance your ability to view these trout in the water. Snow is generally gone and the waters ice-free by July. As this is agricultural water, help protect water quality by packing out trash. The surrounding habitats of the Grand Mesa offer outstanding wildlife viewing all four seasons of the year, particularly good birdwatching spring through fall, and a wonderful summer bloom of wildflowers.

Ownership: USFS (Grand Mesa Visitor Center, 970-856-4153; Grand Valley Ranger District, 970-242-8211; State of Colorado, private water associations

Size: 80 acres

Closest town: Mesa, 26 miles; Cedaredge, 17 miles; Collbran, 23 miles; lodging, restaurants

Directions: *See map previous page*

The Colorado River cutthroat trout is one of the few native trout species remaining in Colorado. Like introduced trout such as rainbow, brook, and brown trout, it provides excellent recreation for anglers.
COLORADO DIVISION OF WILDLIFE

COLORADO PLATEAU

Description: Riparian community of cottonwoods, willows, and tamarisk (which is targeted for eradication) along the Gunnison River and Roubideau Creek. Established windbreaks of juniper and sumac, grain food plots for waterfowl. Surrounding agricultural land and semi-desert shrublands. Wetlands and ponds on the property are recharged from irrigation water and natural recharge from surface and groundwater. www.wildlife.state.co.us

Viewing information: A variety of birds use these riparian bottomlands including orioles, goldfinches, migrating warblers, blue grosbeaks, flycatchers, woodpeckers, owls. Great blue heron nesting colony can be seen. The creek bottom near the confluence of Roubideau Creek and the Gunnison River offers excellent mule deer habitat. The Hamilton and Lower Roubideau tracts are closed to public access March 5 through July 31 to protect nesting waterfowl. A viewing overlook is planned along G Road where visitors can watch habitat reclamation in progress, including tamarisk eradication efforts, wetlands construction, and recovery work on threatened and endangered Colorado River fishes like Colorado pikeminnow (formerly Colorado squawfish), humpback chub, and razorback sucker.

Ownership: CDOW (970-252-6000)

Size: 3,500 acres

Closest town: Delta, 5.75 miles; lodging, restaurants

Directions: See map this page

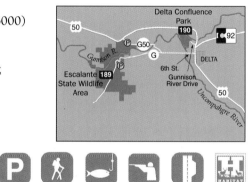

We are connected in so many ways, there's no need to share a sandwich to prove it.

Description: This city park occupies reclaimed land at the confluence of the Uncompahgre and Gunnison Rivers. Best wildlife viewing is along the trail that follows the Gunnison River to the confluence, then along the Uncompahgre River, which is more channelized. Riverine vegetation includes cottonwoods, tamarisk, sumac, and willows. Park also contains constructed ponds lined with cattails.

Viewing information: Lots of beaver activity along the rivers. Good-sized great blue heron nest colony in large cottonwoods on private property on the north side of the Gunnison River, visible from the parking area. Good chance to view a variety of songbirds along the trail, especially along the Gunnison River portion. Orioles, goldfinches, yellow warblers, flycatchers, woodpeckers, wrens. In winter, hundreds of geese use the ponds in the park as loafing areas. Some other waterfowl can be seen. Fort Uncompahgre is a reconstructed living history site within the park with interpreters in period costume. The fort is open April to October 10 a.m. to 4 p.m., Tuesday through Saturday. There is a fee for the fort, but not the park.

Ownership: Town of Delta (970-874-0923)

Size: 265 acres   **Closest town:** Delta, in town; lodging, restaurants

Directions: See map opposite page

The Bullock's oriole inhabits streamside woodlands throughout the state. Look for the long, woven nests dangling like pouches from tree branches. ROBERT E. BARBER

COLORADO PLATEAU

Description: The hatchery lies along the banks of the North Fork of the Gunnison River at the bottom of a small canyon. Surrounding hillsides mainly sagebrush with small spring seeps. Orchards and agricultural land on the mesa around the site. The hatchery has 32 outdoor raceways, six small ponds, and 24 indoor tanks. **www.fws.gov**

Viewing information: View hatchery operations showing all aspects of trout culture, primarily rainbow and cutthroat. Annual production of 2.4 million trout. See fish at all stages, from eggs to catchable trout of 10-inch length. Best time to view hatchery operations is winter, spring, and early summer. Small visitor center with viewing window. Visitors may walk through the hatchery facilities. Good viewing in the area for birds, mule deer, bald eagles in winter and spring. A pair of red-tailed hawks nests on adjacent cliffs. Hatchery open for viewing daylight to dusk; visitor center open 7:30 a.m. to 4 p.m. daily.

Ownership: USFWS (970-872-3170)

Size: 70 acres

Closest town: Hotchkiss, 3 miles; lodging, restaurants

Directions: See map this page

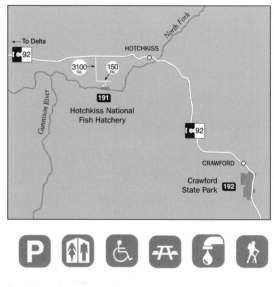

The bald eagle, America's national symbol, gains its distinctive white head and white tail plumage by age five. Hundreds of bald eagles winter in Colorado. Nesting pairs are uncommon but increasing in number.
DAVID F. TONEY

Description: The park surrounds a 406-acre reservoir along Iron Creek. Most of the rocky sandstone shoreline is cottonwood riparian habitat. Uplands on west and north sides are semi-desert shrublands of big sagebrush, rabbitbrush, and cactus intermixed with piñon-juniper woodlands. Uplands on east and south sides are dryland and irrigated grasslands. Cottonwoodlands along the creek traverse the canyon bottom below the dam. **www.parks.state.co.us**

Viewing information: Geese, ducks, and shorebirds of all types use the lake, beach, and lake edges. Migratory songbirds are abundant. Best viewing is spring through fall. Watch for mule deer, coyotes, rabbits, raccoons, and skunks year-round, elk in late fall, and ground squirrels, marmots, and mice spring through fall. Small mammals attract golden eagles and numerous raptors—harriers, kestrels, rough-legged, sharp-shinned, and red-tailed hawks. Also great horned, western screech, and (rarely) northern pygmy owls. Bald eagles and osprey seen early spring and late fall. Frogs, toads, horned and fence lizards, garter snakes, and racers. Visitor center on east side of reservoir along Colorado Highway 92 with interpretive exhibits, brochures, book sales. The Indian Fire Nature Trail, a half-mile long, on west side traverses cottonwoodlands and piñon-juniper hillside. Universally accessible trail on east side starts at the swim beach below the visitor center and continues 0.75 mile around Clear Fork campground.

Ownership: BOR, State Parks (970-921-5721)

Size: 740 acres

Closest town: Crawford, 1 mile; lodging, restaurants

Directions: *See map opposite page*

Western screech owls inhabit southeastern Colorado and western valleys. Because they are small and well camouflaged, you are unlikely to see them. Instead, listen for their distinctive nighttime calls, a series of one-note hoots increasing in tempo.
SHERM SPOELSTRA

COLORADO PLATEAU

Description: Carved by the Gunnison River, this national park features an awesome canyon with rocky walls rising over 2,000 feet in places. Much of the area is oak/serviceberry brushland, with some piñon-juniper woodlands. Douglas-fir and some aspen are found in side canyons, with riparian vegetation along the river. Inquire at the visitor center for specific, up-to-date viewing opportunities. **www.nps.gov**

Viewing information: Hiking the Warner Point Trail or North Rim Campground is possibly the best way to see a variety of birds: ruby-crowned kinglets, mountain chickadees, western tanagers, hairy woodpeckers, Cooper's hawks, and an occasional golden eagle. Green-tailed towhees are common at the south rim campground, along with dusky grouse and various nesting warblers. Near East Portal, dippers can be seen along the river. Watch also for nesting yellow warblers, broad-tailed hummingbirds, and other songbirds. Doves, flickers, Steller's and scrub jays, and other birds are visible from the roads. From the overlooks watch for ravens, turkey vultures, white-throated swifts, violet-green swallows, and golden eagles. Bald eagles are common in spring and fall. You may see endangered peregrine falcons which nest in the park. Mule deer can be easily seen at dusk and early morning along both rims and in the campgrounds. Occasional elk, bighorn sheep, and black bears. Watch for numerous small mammals—chipmunks, ground squirrels, porcupines, marmots, rabbits, skunks.

Ownership: NPS (970-641-2337)

Size: 20,766 acres

Closest town: Montrose, 12.5 miles; restaurants, lodging

Directions: *See map this page*

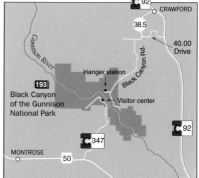

Nimble American dippers entertain wildlife viewers by plunging underwater into rushing streams while searching for insects. They bob and dip when standing on the shore. When airborne, these "water ouzels" fly close to the stream surface.
DENNIS HENRY

202

Description: This scenic drive follows the Uncompahgre River through piñon/juniper-dotted hillsides, cattle ranches, and alfalfa and hay fields. Cottonwood riparian zones occur along the river, and rugged, rocky cliffs near Ouray. Billy Creek State Wildlife Area and Ridgway State Park are along the route. Both are excellent deer and elk viewing sites. A partially paved bike path from Montrose to Ridgway Reservoir features interpretive signs and offers a good chance to view a variety of species.

Viewing information: Mule deer are visible year-round all along the route. There is a chance of seeing bighorn sheep in the Ouray area. Elk can be seen in winter along the highway from Ridgway to Ouray. Watch for bald eagles along the river in winter; golden eagles and red-tailed and other hawks year-round. Sandhill cranes fly over the area in spring and fall. Watch for black swifts high over Ouray, at the head of Box Canyon and along the switchbacks of U.S. Highway 550 south of Ouray. Look for prairie dogs, marmots, and coyotes in open areas. Many songbirds use the riparian zones along the river. Keep an eye open for great blue herons and other wading birds. Elk are abundant between Colona and Ridgway.

Ownership: PVT, CDOW, BLM, USFS (970-249-3711)

Size: 35-mile drive

Closest town: Montrose; Ridgway; Ouray; restaurants, lodging

Directions: See map this page

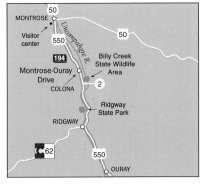

Red-tailed hawks have broad wings, an eerie and shrill cry, and a wide, rounded reddish tail. It's common to see the hawks being mobbed by smaller birds defending their territories and young.
JUDD COONEY

COLORADO PLATEAU

203

Description: This state park surrounds a 1,000-acre reservoir. Outstanding riparian habitat at the south end of the park, where Dallas Creek enters the Uncompahgre River, and at the north end, where Cow Creek flows into the river. Cottonwoods, willows, and wetlands vegetation. Shrublands on surrounding hillsides of Gambel oak and sagebrush. Grasslands dominate lower elevations, with piñon-juniper woodlands covering the upper mesas. www.parks.state.co.us

Viewing information: Late fall and winter are best viewing times for mule deer and elk. Black bear and mountain lion occasionally seen. Bald and golden eagles are common. Park staff operates an eagle feeding station south of the visitor center. Other raptors include ospreys, harriers, and great horned owls; red-tailed, rough-legged, sharp-shinned, and Cooper's hawks. Wild turkeys sometimes seen in fall and winter. Crows, ravens, magpies, flickers, swallows, bluebirds, finches, and hummingbirds all common, as well as Steller's, scrub and pinyon jays. Small mammals include beavers, marmots, skunks, rabbits, chipmunks, foxes, coyotes, and porcupines. Visitor center with bookstore, interactive displays, interpretive program. Bird list, guided nature walks, self-guided nature trail, interpretive signs, viewing decks.

Ownership: State Parks (970-626-5822), BOR

Size: 2,200 acres

Closest town: Ridgway, 5 miles; lodging, restaurants

Directions: See map opposite page

Red foxes are intelligent, adaptable, opportunistic, and not picky about what they eat. This ability to take advantage of a wide array of circumstances and food means red foxes are found throughout Colorado in almost every habitat. CLAUDE STEELMAN

Description: Split among five tracts, this wildlife area varies in elevation from 6,800 to 8,200 feet. The lower reaches are irrigated hay meadows with piñon-juniper woodlands intermixed with oakbrush and shrublands of mountain-mahogany, three-leaf sumac, and other shrubs. Spruce-fir forest at higher elevations. Narrowleaf cottonwood riparian habitat along Billy Creek. www.wildlife.state.co.us

Viewing information: Excellent winter viewing of elk and bald and golden eagles. Up to 800 elk winter in the meadows along Billy Creek and eagles, especially bald eagles, are commonly seen in the narrowleaf cottonwoods along the creek. The property is closed from January 1 to March 31 to protect wintering elk and deer, though the viewing platform will remain open. The area is heavily used by fall hunters. Nearby **Owl Creek Pass** is good for mountain birds, elk, deer, and small mammals.

Ownership: CDOW (970-252-6000)

Size: 7,500 acres

Closest town: Ridgway, 10 miles; lodging, restaurants

Directions: See map this page

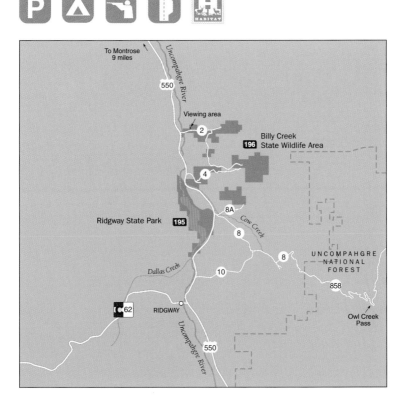

COLORADO PLATEAU

Description: Rolling hills with sagebrush and high-desert shrublands, uplands covered with dense stands of piñon-juniper woodland. Thirty miles of riparian habitat along Disappointment Creek.

Viewing information: The valley offers good wildlife viewing late fall and winter due to high concentrations of large mammals and raptors. It is crucial winter range for deer and elk. Pronghorn also can be seen. Watch for golden and bald eagles; this area has the highest concentration of wintering bald eagles in southern Colorado. A variety of raptors prey upon small mammals in the area, including prairie dogs, chipmunks, jackrabbits, and cottontails. Watch also for coyotes and foxes. Check ponds and waterways for beavers, muskrats, and a variety of waterfowl. The **Dry Creek Basin State Wildlife Area** (Habitat Stamp required) lies about 10 miles farther east on Colorado Highway 141. Check the Dry Creek Basin kiosk, at Basin on the southeast side of CO 141 and 12 miles south of CO 145, for further interpretive information.

Ownership: BLM (970-247-4874)

Size: 40,000 acres

Closest town: Naturita, 15 miles

Directions: *See map this page*

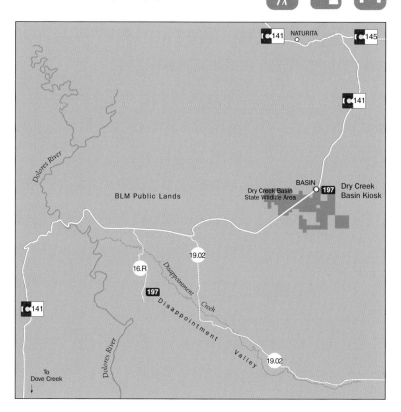

Description: Wetlands of sedges and a few cattails within a 20-acre enclosure, with a small body of open water, set within an open meadow in mountain forest. Beyond the large open park is ponderosa pine forest with a rich understory of oak, aspen, rose, snowberries, and flowering plants. Potholes were created by the USDA Forest Service to improve waterfowl habitat and the site is fenced to protect the wetlands from livestock grazing. **www.fs.fed.us**

Viewing information: The wetlands attract a good variety of waterfowl, both in migration and nesting. Watch for dabbling ducks such as pintails, gadwalls, mallards, and cinnamon and green-winged teal. Canada geese, coots, and eared grebes are also seen. Mule deer and elk are often seen drinking at the lake. Enter through either of the steel gates, one on the east end and one on the west end. There is no trail but the terrain is open and flat. Watch for Abert's squirrels, pygmy nuthatches, wild turkeys, and other pine forest dwellers in the surrounding ponderosa pine woodlands.

Ownership: USFS (970-882-7296)

Size: 30 acres

Closest town: Dove Creek, 25 miles; lodging, restaurants

Directions: See map this page

Wild turkeys forage on the ground for acorns, seeds, insects, and other food. At night they roost together in groups in the tops of trees. They are generally found in pine forests of southern Colorado as well as along cottonwoodlands of waterways in eastern Colorado.
CLAUDE STEELMAN

COLORADO PLATEAU

207

Description: Ponderosa pine, piñon-juniper habitat, large meadows and riparian areas. The canyon is 1,000 feet deep and fairly broad near the dam, becoming steep-sided at the lower end with up to twelve geologic layers visible. The first 12 miles of the road, from McPhee Dam to Bradfield Bridge, are passable by passenger car, though closed to motor vehicles December 1 through March 31 to protect wintering deer and elk. Access is open to ski or foot traffic. The next 19 miles, from the bridge to Dove Creek Pumps, are passable only by foot or horseback after high water recedes (mid-June). Good rafting from Memorial Day through mid-June. The last 28 miles, from the pumps to Slick Rock, are passable by four-wheel-drive the first 13 miles; by foot, horse, and mountain bike the last 15 miles. **www.blm.gov**

Viewing information: In spring watch for deer, elk, wild turkeys, and an array of meadow and woodland songbirds. River otters in the river and along the bank. Bears and sign of bobcats and mountain lions may be seen in summer. Brown, rainbow, and Snake River cutthroat trout visible in pools. Bald eagles in winter, peregrine falcons in summer, and golden eagles are viewed year-round. Wild turkeys move to and from the river in morning and evening. Desert bighorn sheep inhabit the steep lower section.

Ownership: USFS (970-882-7276), BLM, PVT, BOR (970-247-4082)

Size: 55 miles of river canyon

Closest town: Dove Creek, 15 miles; restaurants, lodging

Directions: *See map this page*

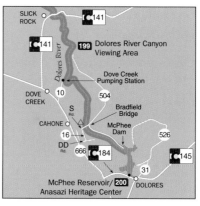

Southwest Colorado's Dolores River Canyon offers wild country, ample recreational opportunities, and a strong sampling of the state's excellent wildlife viewing.
ROBERT E. BARBER

Description: A flooded river canyon with a sloping, timbered shore and several side canyons. McPhee is the second largest reservoir in the state. Shores are winter range for deer and elk. Surrounding slopes support piñon-juniper and Douglas-fir woodlands with cultivated fields (some planted with alfalfa and grasses for wildlife forage). Surrounding wildlife management areas closed December 1 to March 31.

Viewing information: Self-guided boat tour brochure highlights viewing opportunities along McPhee's fifty miles of shoreline. Numerous waterfowl and waterbirds on the lake. Canada geese, mergansers, coots, and a variety of ducks seen year-round. Look for mountain bluebirds, kingfishers, Steller's jays, rock squirrels, and muskrats. Wintering bald eagles and migrant osprey. An osprey nesting platform has been erected in hopes of attracting these 'fishhawks' to nest. Predators include great horned owls, bobcats, and coyotes. The **Anasazi Heritage Center**, three miles from Dolores, is a good place to see elk December through February. Deer are abundant. Watch for raptors, particularly bald eagles, from the mesa edges. There is a universally accessible nature trail that is good for wildlife viewing.

Ownership: BOR, BLM (970-385-6577), USFS (970-882-7296)

Size: 50 miles of shoreline

Closest town: Dolores; restaurants, lodging

Directions: See map opposite page

Redheads are diving ducks often confused with canvasbacks, whose heads are similarly colored. But the canvasback has a sloping head, while the redhead sports a distinctly round profile. DENNIS HENRY

COLORADO PLATEAU

209

Found in prairie dog colonies where they nest in abandoned burrows, burrowing owls are small-bodied and long-legged. The birds can usually be spotted standing on the ground or on fenceposts. TOM TIETZ

Description: The cliff dwellings of the Ancestral Puebloans highlight this dramatic country of flat-topped mesas, steep canyons, and wonderful vistas. Mesa country terrain includes piñon-juniper with oakbrush, shrubs, and Douglas-fir in the draws, and sagebrush valleys below. Check at the visitor center for current viewing opportunities. **www.nps.gov**

Viewing information: The park's twisting canyons and rugged terrain offer good raptor viewing. Eagles, hawks, and vultures are visible soaring on thermal updrafts along the mesa's escarpment. The Knife Edge Trail has views of peregrine falcons and golden eagles, as well as red-tailed, Cooper's, and sharp-shinned hawks. Bald eagles and rough-legged hawks are seen in winter. The museum patio is a good place to watch hummingbirds. Mule deer are very common throughout the park. Prater Canyon is a good stop to view deer as well as wild turkeys. Spruce Tree Point features a turkey vulture roost. Look for ravens at Navajo Canyon Overlook and Soda Canyon, and white-throated swifts at Cliff Palace Dwelling. Watch among the piñon pines for scrub, pinyon, and Steller's jays. Carnivores sometimes seen along the park entrance road include coyotes, gray foxes, and an occasional black bear and mountain lion.

Ownership: NPS (970-529-4465)

Size: 52,000 acres

Closest town: Cortez, 10 miles; restaurants, lodging

Directions: *See map this page*

While justifiably famous for its ancient Indian ruins, Mesa Verde National Park also provides wonderful wildlife viewing. This spectacular land of canyons and mesas is in the Four Corners region.
DAN PEHA

COLORADO PLATEAU

Index — Popular Species

Here are suggestions of where to view some of Colorado's most popular wildlife species. These aren't the only places they can be viewed, but these sites offer good opportunities to see these species. The numbers listed below are page numbers.

Index — Sites